The Rhythms of
Jewish Living

A Sephardic Exploration
of Judaism's Spirituality

Rabbi Marc D. Angel, PhD

For People of All Faiths, All Backgrounds

JEWISH LIGHTS Publishing

The Rhythms of Jewish Living:
A Sephardic Exploration of Judaism's Spirituality

© 2015 by Marc D. Angel

Originally published by Sepher-Hermon Press.

Library of Congress Cataloging-in-Publication Data
Angel, Marc, author.
  The rhythms of Jewish living : a Sephardic exploration of Judaism's spirituality / Rabbi Marc D. Angel, PhD.
      pages cm
  "Original title: The rhythms of Jewish living : a Sephardic approach, published in 1986"—ECIP data view.
  Includes bibliographical references and index.
  ISBN 978-1-58023-834-2 (pbk.)—ISBN 978-1-58023-841-0 (ebook) 1. Judaism—Essence, genius, nature. 2. Sephardim. I. Title.
  BM565.A73 2015
  296.7—dc23
                                2015008787

ISBN 978-1-68336-420-7 (hc)

Manufactured in the United States of America
Cover design: Tim Holtz
Interior design: Michael J. Myers
Cover art: ©2010 Alan A. Tobey / iStockphoto

For People of All Faiths, All Backgrounds
Jewish Lights Publishing
An Imprint of Turner Publishing Company
Tel: (615) 255-2665
www.jewishlights.com

In appreciation of my loving family and friends,
who have made life's adventure so wondrous

Contents

Preface

A midrash teaches that the way of Torah is a narrow path. On the right is fire and on the left is ice. If one veers from the path, one will be destroyed by either the fire or the ice.

The Torah way of life is balanced, harmonious, and sensible. It imbues life with depth, meaning, and true happiness. Yet it has not always been easy for people to stay on the path. Veering to the left freezes the soul of Judaism. Classic Judaism expresses itself through the Bible, Jewish law, and rabbinic teachings. These are the source of its warmth and harmony. They imbue the rhythms of Jewish living. When one abandons Jewish belief and observance, this is a turn toward the ice. Inevitably, this leads to a breakdown in Jewish experience and Jewish identity. In veering to the right of the path of Torah, one faces the spiritual destruction of fire—excessive zeal, religious extremism. This tendency manifests itself in a spirit of isolationism, self-righteousness, and xenophobia. It reduces the Torah way of life to self-imposed physical and spiritual ghettos.

This book seeks to present a viable framework for a balanced and harmonious understanding of Judaism's way of life. It steers a course that avoids the ice on the left and the fire on the right.

Note: Throughout the text of this book, I refer to God as "He." God, of course, is neither masculine nor feminine; whatever pronouns or adjectives we use in relation to the Almighty are all to be understood as symbolic, not literal. I follow the classic biblical, liturgical, and rabbinic imagery of God that prevails in the source material I quote in this book.

My hope is that this book will open a new window of understanding of Judaism for its readers. If so, my labor is well rewarded.

Marc D. Angel

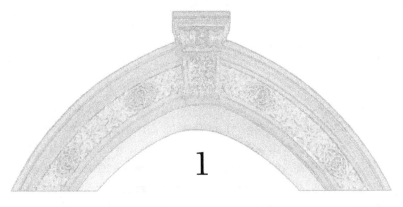

1

THE RHYTHMS
OF NATURE

Creation

To a religious person, the universe is filled with hidden voices and secret meanings. The natural world, being the creation of God, signals the awesomeness of its Creator.

The Torah opens with the dramatic words, "In the beginning, God created the heavens and the earth." It does not begin with the story of God's revelation to the Israelites at Sinai, nor with specific commandments. The first chapter of Genesis establishes in powerful terms that God created the universe and everything within it.

An ancient Aramaic translation of the Torah interprets the Hebrew word *b'reishit* (in the beginning) to mean *behokhmah* (with wisdom).[1] According to this translation, the Torah opens with the statement, "With wisdom did God create the heavens and the earth." A human being, by recognizing the vast wisdom of God as reflected in the universe He created, comes to a profound awareness of her relationship with God. Indeed, experiencing God as Creator is the beginning of religious wisdom.

Moses Maimonides, the preeminent Jewish thinker of the Middle Ages, has understood this truth. He wrote:

> Now what is the way that leads to the love of Him and the reverence for Him? When a person contemplates His great and

1

wondrous acts and creations, obtaining from them a glimpse of His wisdom, which is beyond compare and infinite, he will promptly love and glorify Him, longing exceedingly to know the great Name of God, as David said: "My whole being thirsts for God, the living God" (Psalm 42:3). When he ponders over these very subjects, he will immediately recoil, startled, conceiving that he is a lowly, obscure creature ... as David said: "As I look up to the heavens Your fingers made ... what is man that you should think of him?" (Psalm 8:4-5).[2]

The source of the love and fear of God rests in the contemplation of the world that God created.

The Torah and the Natural Universe

By opening with the story of Creation, the Torah teaches that a person must have a living relationship with the natural world in order to enter into and maintain a living relationship with God. Jewish spirituality flowers and deepens through this relationship. The ancient sacred texts of Judaism, beginning with the Torah itself, guide us to live with a keen awareness of the rhythms of nature.

Jewish spirituality is organically linked to the natural rhythms of the universe. To a great extent, Jewish religious traditions serve to bring Jews into a sensitive relationship with the natural world. Many commandments and customs lead in this direction, drawing out the love and reverence that emerge from the contemplation of God's creations.

An ancient teaching is that God "looked into the Torah and created the world."[3] This statement reflects a belief that the Torah actually predated Creation and served as the blueprint for the universe. This enigmatic teaching has been subject to various interpretations. But perhaps its main intent is to reveal the organic connection between the Torah and the universe. Since the laws of the Torah are linked to nature, it is as though nature was created to fit these laws. The natural world was created in harmony with the revealed words of the Torah. A Talmudic statement teaches that God created the world only on the condition that Israel would accept the Torah. If not, the world would again be reduced to chaos and void.[4]

The Talmud teaches that God gave the people of Israel 613 commandments (*Makkot* 23b). There are 248 positive commandments, corresponding to the number of limbs in the human body. And there are 365 negative commandments, corresponding to the number of days in the solar year. This means that the Torah's commandments are ingrained in our very being: in our limbs, in the years of our lives. God's original design in Creation was related to His original design of the Torah and its commandments. The natural universe and the spiritual universe are in rhythm with each other.

This harmony may also be implicit in the blessing recited after reading from the Torah. The blessing extols God "who has given us His Torah, the Torah of truth, and has planted within us eternal life (*hayyei olam*)." The phrase *hayyei olam* has been understood to refer to the eternal soul of each person, or to the Torah, which is the source of eternal life for the people of Israel. Yet perhaps the blessing also suggests another dimension of meaning.

The world *olam* in biblical Hebrew usually refers to time—a long duration, eternity. In later Hebrew, *olam* came to mean "the world"—referring to space rather than specifically to time. *Hayyei olam*, therefore, may be understood as "eternal life," but also as "the life of the world." The blessing may be echoing both meanings. Aside from relating to eternal life, the blessing might be understood as praising God for planting within us the life of the world. That is, through His Torah, God has tied our lives to the rhythms of the natural world. Through this connection with the natural world, we are brought into a living relationship with God.

Jewish tradition thus has two roads to God: the natural world, which reveals God as Creator; and the Torah, which records the words of God to the people of Israel. But the Torah itself leads us back to the first road, the road of experiencing God as Creator. The Torah and nature are bound together.

The relationship of Torah and nature is evident in Psalm 19. This psalm has played an important role in Jewish religious consciousness, since it is included in the Sabbath liturgy and is read daily in some communities. The psalm has two distinct parts that at first glance seem to be unconnected. It begins:

> The heavens declare the glory of God,
>   and the firmament tells His handiwork.
> Day unto day utters the tale,
>   night unto night unfolds knowledge.
> There is no word, no speech,
>   their voice is not heard,
> yet their course extends through all the world,
>   and their theme to the end of the world.

The psalm goes on to describe the sun, which rejoices as a strong man prepared to run his course:

> Its setting forth is from one end of the skies,
>   its circuit unto the other extreme,
> and nothing is hidden from its heat.

Then the psalm makes an abrupt shift. It continues:

> The law of the Lord is perfect,
>   comforting the soul....
> The precepts of the Lord are right,
>   rejoicing the heart.
> The commandment of the Lord is clear,
>   enlightening the eyes.

From a description of the glory of God as manifested in the natural world, the psalm jumps to a praise of the Torah, God's special revelation to the people of Israel.

The psalm seems to be composed of two separate segments, as if accidentally put together by a careless editor. But the psalm in its present form has been part of the Jewish religious tradition for thousands of years. Its impact on Jews has been as a unitary literary piece.

The enigma of this psalm's organization is easily solved. Psalm 19 is teaching that one may come to an understanding of God both through the natural world and through the Torah. God has given us two roads to Him.

This concept underlies the organization of Jewish prayers for both the morning and evening services. In both of these services, the recitation of the *Sh'ma*—the biblical passage proclaiming the unity of God—is a central feature. In each service, the *Sh'ma* is introduced by two sections, each concluding with a blessing. Although the words of these sections vary between the two services, their themes are the same. The first section praises God as Creator, the One who called the universe into being, who set the sun, moon, and stars in their rhythms, who separated day and night. The second section praises God as the giver of the Torah, as the One who loves Israel. Only after reciting both sections do we recite the *Sh'ma* and the subsequent prayers. The God of creation and the God of revelation are One, and we may find our way to Him through His world of creation and through His revealed word.

Sunrise

Certain moments in the day are particularly conducive to pensiveness. At dawn, with the rising of the sun, the sky in the east awakens with color and light. At sunrise, one experiences the still-fading darkness of night along with the faintly emerging light of day. It is an in-between time, vague, pregnant with possibility.

Jewish tradition has long taught that the ideal time for morning prayer is at sunrise. It is considered particularly virtuous to pray at that time, when the prayer is in harmony with the emerging sun. The prayer of the morning extols God, who "in His goodness ever revives each day anew His work of creation." The rising sun is symbolic of this daily re-creation of the universe. At the very moment when the sun rises and the world seems to be re-created—that is the preferred moment for the morning prayer. In that mysterious, quiet, in-between time, we experience God the Creator both in the skies and in the words of our prayer book.

Sunset

Sundown, too, is a mysterious and poetic time. The sun is dropping out of sight. The sky in the west is streaked with red and purple. In a short while, the world will be plunged into darkness.

Again, Jewish tradition has understood the connection of human spirituality with the natural world. Jewish law prescribes that the afternoon prayers be recited before the sun sets. Many Jews recite the afternoon prayers just as the sun is setting. The night prayers are to be said ideally when the stars in the sky can be seen.

The daily prayer rhythm brings the worshipper into the natural rhythm of sunrise and sunset.

Midnight

The power of night, especially before the development of electric lights, was enormous. Without streetlights and other artificial lighting, the darkness of night is awesome, frightening. The cycle of light and darkness profoundly affected the lives of almost everyone. During the day, people would be able to be outdoors, work, tend the farm, visit friends and neighbors. But at night, the fear of darkness took hold. People preferred to remain in their homes, in their enclosed world of relative safety.

The darkness of night, in spite of the fear it can engender, also presents a remarkable unfolding of God's creation: the stars. A person may enhance his spiritual life by going outside at night and gazing at the stars. This experience will cause one to fall into a state of awe and wonder. One will appreciate the greatness of God and feel the elevation of the soul.

Midnight, as the furthest point into the darkness, is a particularly haunting time. Kabbalists connected their spirituality to midnight. Rabbi Abraham Halevy, of sixteenth-century Safed, reported that the pious Jews of his town would awaken each night in order to recite a special set of prayers at midnight. They sat on the ground, wrapped in black, and lamented the destruction of the ancient Temple in Jerusalem.[5] At midnight, the darkest moment in the daily cycle, the mystics cried and prayed over the darkest moment in the spiritual life of the Jewish people. But the lamentations, with all their sadness, were also imbued with hope. After all, midnight was the furthest one could fall into darkness. From then on, the movement was toward sunrise, toward redemption.

The mystics associated the experiences of the Jewish people with the cycle of the sun. To this day, the midnight vigil—known as *Tikkun Hatsot*—is observed among pious Jews.

The Moon

The religious mind has always been intrigued by the heavens above. Religious language speaks of "our God in heaven," "our Father in heaven." Heaven may be understood allegorically—i.e., God is transcendent, beyond reach. The fact that religious imagery places God in heaven reflects a deep religious sentiment that God is experienced by our musings about heaven. Humans entertain thoughts of God's transcendence upon contemplating the sun, stars, and moon of the heavens.

While the daily cycle is governed by sunrise and sunset, the monthly cycle is the domain of the moon. Mircea Eliade, the noted religious anthropologist, has observed that "it is through the moon's phases—that is, its birth, death, and resurrection—that men came to know at once their own mode of being in the cosmos and the chances for their survival or rebirth."[6]

Lunar symbolism has had a profound place in religious thought. Eliade suggests that it enabled people to connect such heterogeneous things as birth, becoming, death, and resurrection; the waters, plants, woman, fecundity, and immortality; cosmic darkness, prenatal existence, life after death, and rebirth; fate, temporality, and death; and others. The moon is symbolic of human life. Its rhythmic cycles keep it ever changing. It has a dark, unknown side. And even its light is muted and mysterious.

Professor Gershom Scholem commented on the role of the moon in kabbalistic thought: "No cosmic event seemed to the kabbalists to be more closely connected with the exile of all things, with the imperfection and the taint inherent in all Being, than this periodic lessening of the moon."[7] Scholem points out the striking convergence of two themes which were to dominate the Kabbalah from the sixteenth century on: the catastrophe of exile and the regeneration of the light after its total disappearance. The moon, in its waning, symbolized exile into darkness. But the same moon, in its rebirth, symbolized the promise that all things would one day be rectified through redemption.

In ancient Israel, the day of the new moon (Rosh Hodesh) was celebrated as a joyous festival. When the great rabbinical court functioned in Jerusalem during the days of the Temple, witnesses who sighted the beginnings of the moon would come to court and testify concerning their sighting. The court would then declare that the new month had begun. A celebration was held in honor of all those who came to testify.

The Jewish festivals and holy days were determined by the court's declaration of the new moon, based on the testimony of reliable witnesses. Thus, Israelites would search the heavens for the sign of the emerging moon, since the moon was so important to their religious calendar. Rosh Hodesh has continued to be observed as a minor festival throughout the centuries, including our own day.

The mystics of sixteenth-century Safed attached great significance to Rosh Hodesh. They also observed the day preceding the new moon as a fast day to be devoted to meditation on the themes of exile and redemption. This day became known as Yom Kippur Katan, the minor day of atonement.

One of the mystics, Rabbi Abraham Galante, listed rules for the pious people to follow.[8] Among them, he described the practices observed on the day prior to the new moon. Everyone fasted—men, women, and young students. They gathered in one place and remained there all day reciting penitential prayers and confessions, and also giving each other lashes. Some people placed large rocks on their stomachs, symbolic of the fact that they considered themselves guilty of crimes punishable by stoning; some choked themselves with their hands. Some climbed into sacks and had someone drag them around the synagogue. On the eve of the new moon, some had the custom of arising at midnight to read from the book of Psalms. These observances, though tending to be ascetic, demonstrated the connection between the spirituality of the people and the rhythm of the moon. The moon itself became a feature of their religious life.

A widely observed practice to this day is the recitation of a special blessing upon witnessing the moon in its brightness and its fullness. The proper time for this blessing is on a night between the seventh and fifteenth days of the lunar cycle. In many communities it has been customary to recite this blessing on a Saturday night, after the conclusion of Shabbat. At that time people are still dressed in their Shabbat clothes and are still imbued with the joy of Shabbat. The blessing over the moon is to be recited on a clear night when the moon is visible, not hidden behind clouds.

The Talmud reports the opinion of Rabbi Aha bar Hanina, who stated in the name of Rabbi Asi, who stated in the name of Rabbi Yohanan: "One who blesses the new moon at the proper time is as one who has received the Divine Presence" (*Sanhedrin* 42a). Rabbi David Abudraham, the medieval Spanish-Jewish commentator on the prayer book, explained this Talmudic passage as follows: Even though God is not seen by the human eye, He is seen by means of His marvels and wonders. He reveals Himself to us by means of the renewal of the moon.[9]

The blessing over the moon is generally accompanied by the chanting of certain psalms and biblical verses. The text of the blessing is:

Blessed are You, Lord our God, King of the universe,
who created the heavens with His word,
and with the breath of His mouth all their host.
He gave them a decree and a time that they not change their
  appointed task.
They rejoice and are glad to do the will of their Master.
He is a true worker whose works are truth.
And to the moon He said that it should be renewed,
a crown of beauty for the ones carried from the womb,
who, in the future, will be renewed (like the moon)
to thank their Creator because of the glory of His kingdom.
Blessed are You, God, renewer of the months.

This blessing expresses the recognition that God created the heavenly spheres and set them into an eternal pattern. The moon is described as a crown of beauty for human beings, a symbol of the renewal that we will experience. The moon, in some ways, is a prefiguration of human experience.

The blessing for the new moon is generally recited outdoors in the presence of a quorum of at least ten men. It is in no way to be considered as moon worship, but rather as worship of God inspired by the regularity and the mystery of the moon. The blessing of the moon concludes with a quotation from the Talmud: "It was taught in the school of Rabbi Ishmael that if the children of Israel would be received by their Father in heaven only once a month, it would be enough. Said Abbaye, Let us stand in reverence when we thank God for the new moon" (*Sanhedrin* 42a).

The Seasons

The seasons of the year influence the foods we eat, the clothes we wear, the activities we perform, and even the way we feel. The yearly cycle of seasons passes from the blossoms of the spring to the heat of the summer to the colorful decline of autumn to the cold of winter.

The biblical festivals occur at the beginning of autumn (Rosh Hashanah, Yom Kippur, Sukkot) and at the beginning of spring (Passover). Shavuot, which is only a one-day festival in Israel and a two-day observance in the diaspora, occurs seven weeks after the second night of Passover and is connected to the Passover festival by the counting of the omer. All of these festivals are linked to the harvests of autumn and spring, natural times for human beings to rejoice and express thanksgiving to God.

There may be an additional spiritual message in the timing of the festivals. Spring is the season of rebirth and promise; autumn is the beginning of decline and points to future desolation. Summer and winter are the extreme seasons, while spring and autumn are transitional seasons. It is in autumn and spring that we are most aware of the process of nature, when we see its changes before our eyes. And it is in times of transition and change when the power of God is most apparent.

An Autumn Fire Festival

In chapter 3, we will discuss the significance of the festivals. Presently, we are concerned with their relationship to the rhythms of the seasons, to the rhythms of nature. In this connection, it is interesting to consider a special celebration, known as *Simhat Beit Ha-Sho'evah*, held in the ancient Temple in Jerusalem on the night following the first day of Sukkot. Many scholars have believed that it was a water festival involving water libations and prayers to God for an abundance of rainfall during the coming season. Some scholars, however, have suggested that this celebration was actually a fire festival.

The Mishnah describes this celebration as being tremendously joyous. Our sages have stated that "one who has not seen the joy of *Beit Ha-Sho'evah* has not seen joy in his life" (*Sukkah* 5:1) Studying the Mishnah's description of the celebration (*Sukkah* 5) will shed light on its meaning.

The Mishnah relates that at the conclusion of the first day of the holiday, the people gathered in the women's section of the Temple. Young priests would ascend golden candelabra and fill the cups with oil. The wicks used were made from worn-out priestly vestments. When the candelabra were lit, "there was not an alleyway in Jerusalem that was not lit up from the light of *Beit Ha-Sho'evah*." The sages and pious people danced with torches of fire in their hands and sang words of praise to God. The Levites played their harps, lyres, cymbals, trumpets, and innumerable musical instruments while they stood on the fifteen stairs connecting the women's section with the Israelite men's section.

Two priests stood at the upper gate, holding trumpets. The celebration carried on through the night, and at the sound of the crowing of the rooster in the early morning the priests sounded the trumpets. They descended to the tenth step and again sounded the trumpets. When they reached the women's section, they sounded the trumpets a third time. They continued to sound the trumpets until they reached the gate that exited to the east. Having reached that gate, the people turned to the west and said: "Our ancestors who were in this place turned their backs to the ark of God and faced the east, and they bowed eastward to the sun. But we, our eyes face God." Rabbi Yehudah said: They would say: "We are for God, and to God we lift our eyes."

The historian Solomon Zeitlin deduces from the Mishnah that the Israelites during the time of the First Temple used this occasion to bow in an eastward direction toward the rising sun. The Israelites of the Second Temple, though, rejected the custom of their ancestors and specifically turned to the west upon leaving the Temple, keeping their eyes directed to the holy ark, rather than to the sun.[10]

It is clear from the above description that the ceremony had something to do with the sun. The fire and torches that characterized the celebration were symbolic of the sun. Though the Jews of the Second Temple did not bow to the sun, those of the First Temple did do so. In origin, then, the festival was connected to the sun. Why?

An answer may be derived from the biblical verse that describes Sukkot as "the festival of the ingathering at the turn of the year" (Exodus 34:22). The autumn festival occurs at the "turn of the year," when the hours of daylight are declining with each passing day. Going into the autumn, one could easily foresee the arrival of winter, with its very short days and very long nights. The power of the sun might appear to be in decline. Therefore, at this season of the turn of the year, the Israelites connected their religious celebration to the sun. They filled the night with torches and fire, and the sounds of trumpets and music at the time of the rising sun. They proclaimed their faithfulness to God, Creator of the sun. Vestiges of the ancient Temple celebration have continued to exist in various Jewish communities, though the original meaning of the holiday is hardly recognized. It has been customary among Middle Eastern communities to light many lamps in their synagogues in honor of *Simhat Beit Ha-Sho'evah*, and to let the lights glow throughout the night.

Springtime

In the Jewish calendar, the spring season begins with the month of Nissan. This is the time when trees are beginning to blossom and when the natural world is starting to flower with color and new life.

Jewish tradition prescribes that during the month of Nissan Jews should visit orchards or gardens so that they may see trees with new blossoms. This visit is to be done in groups, to lend a communal aspect to the celebration. The blessing to be recited upon seeing trees with new blossoms is:

Blessed are You, Lord our God, King of the universe,
who has not omitted anything from His world,
and has created good creatures and good trees to give pleasure to
* human beings.*

The blessing is in gratitude for the human pleasure derived from observing the beauties of nature. According to Jewish law, this blessing is to be recited only once each year, as a reminder of the yearly renewal of nature that comes about through the power of God. The blessing is to be recited while the tree is newly blossoming, not when fruit has already grown on it. The blessing is not on the fruit but on the renewal of nature, which God brings each springtime.[11]

The Torah refers to Passover as "the spring festival." It must always occur during the springtime. This rule determines calendar calculations. Months are based on a lunar cycle, each month beginning with the new moon. However, the lunar year has only 354 days, compared to the 365 days of the solar calendar. If the Jews followed only the lunar cycle, Passover would not necessarily occur during the springtime. (Muslims do follow a lunar calendar and their holidays are not bound to any season.) The Jewish sages of antiquity devised a cycle in which there are seven leap years during each nineteen-year cycle. Each leap year has one full month added (Second Adar). Thus, the lunar calendar is brought into harmony with the solar calendar and Passover always occurs in the springtime.

Tu B'Shvat

The first mishnah in the Talmudic tractate of Rosh Hashanah refers to the fifteenth day of the month of Shevat (Tu B'Shvat) as the new year for trees. This date marked the starting point for tithing fruits in ancient Israel. The significance of the date expanded over the centuries so that this minor holiday has become associated with a celebration of the abundance of nature. Observances of Tu B'Shvat were broadened under the influence of Rabbi Hayyim Vital and other sixteenth-century Sephardic kabbalists living in Safed. From Safed, these customs spread throughout Asia, North Africa, and Europe.

Tu B'Shvat prayers and readings were arranged in a distinctive order for use in a service. In the mid-eighteenth century, a booklet was published entitled *Peri Ets Hadar* that includes a ritual based on the practices of the kabbalists. It lists many fruits that are to be eaten on this holiday, with special emphasis given to those grown in Israel. The booklet calls for the drinking of four cups of wine as at the traditional Passover seder. A prayer for the people of Israel is recited along with a number of biblical passages that relate to fruit or vegetation.

According to the kabbalists, one should taste at least twelve fruits on Tu B'Shvat. Moroccan Jews customarily eat a minimum of fifteen different fruits. Iraqi celebrations called for serving at least one hundred kinds of fruits, nuts, and vegetables. The text for the occasion includes readings from the Bible, the *Zohar*, and rabbinic writings. A festive meal follows the readings.

The four cups of wine drunk during the service each have their own significance. The first cup is pale white wine. This symbolizes winter and the dormant earth awaiting the planting season. The second cup is more golden in color and represents the time when the earth comes alive and sap starts to flow in the trees. The third cup of wine is a rosé, symbolizing the blossoming of the trees. (In Israel, Tu B'Shvat is associated with the flowering of almond trees.) The final cup of wine is a deep red, symbolizing the land's ripening fruit and its overall fertility.

The Blessing of the Sun

Jewish tradition acknowledges a solar cycle that takes twenty-eight years. According to the biblical account of Creation, the sun was created on the fourth day—Wednesday—at the time of sunrise. The sun's yearly cycle takes 365 and a fourth days. Therefore, the position of the sun at the end of its first anniversary of existence was one-fourth of a day later than its position on the morning of its creation. Each year, it moves an additional quarter of a day. Thus it takes twenty-eight years for the sun to return to the exact position in which it stood on the Wednesday morning when it was first created.

A service and blessing commemorates the creation of the sun once every twenty-eight years at sunrise. The service includes quotations from the Bible relating to the sun. Its main feature is the blessing that states:

> *Blessed are You, Lord our God, King of the universe,*
> *who performs the act of creation.*

Jewish tradition, then, not only ties our spirituality to the daily rhythms of the sun, the monthly rhythms of the moon, the seasonal rhythms of nature, but also to a twenty-eight-year cycle of the sun.

Other Natural Phenomena

Jewish law prescribes a blessing upon seeing a falling star, on experiencing an earthquake, on witnessing lightning and thunder, on observing exceedingly strong winds. On all of these phenomena, the blessing is:

> *Blessed are You, Lord our God, King of the universe,*
> *who performs the act of creation.*

All of these natural phenomena are reflections of the original act of God's creation. An alternative blessing that may also be recited is:

> *Blessed are You, Lord our God, King of the universe,*
> *whose strength and might fill the world.*

Rabbi David Abudraham explained that this blessing praises God for giving nature the power to reveal the ultimate power of the Creator of the universe. By seeing an image of God's strength in the powers of nature, we become awed by God's greatness. (The present custom is to recite the blessing "who performs the act of creation" over lightning and "whose power and might fill the world" over thunder.)

The blessing praising God as the one who performs the act of creation is also recited on seeing an unusual mountain or a desert. These topographical phenomena hark back to the days of Creation, and again remind the viewer of God, the Creator.

Upon seeing a rainbow, one should recite the following blessing:

Blessed are You, Lord our God, King of the universe,
who remembers His covenant [with Noah],
who is trustworthy in His covenant and established in His word.

The Torah describes the rainbow as a sign of God's covenant with His creations on earth that He will never again bring a flood to destroy humanity. It is interesting that God chose the rainbow as a sign for His permanent covenant with humans. A rainbow is intangible, unreachable, and ephemeral. God rests His covenant not in something solid, but in a bodiless rainbow, a colorful arc of vapor refracted in the sunlight. God's power can be seen not only in great mountains and powerful oceans, but also in something as insubstantial and transient as a rainbow.

A Talmudic discussion about rainbows recognizes that this mysterious natural phenomenon is in some way a reflection of God Himself. Rabbi Abba stated that anyone who stares at a rainbow is showing disrespect for God (*Hagigah* 16a). The sage Rava said that anyone who stares at a rainbow is obligated to prostrate himself on the ground. These opinions are based on Ezekiel 1:28, which compares Ezekiel's vision of the brightness around God to the appearance of a rainbow:

As the appearance of the bow that is in the cloud in the day of rain,
so was the appearance of the brightness round about, this was the
appearance of the lightness of the glory of the Lord. And when I
saw it, I fell upon my face and I heard a voice of one that spoke.

The rainbow, therefore, is suggestive of the glory of God Himself, and should inspire within us a sense of awe and mystery.

Psalm 19

We return to the first verses of Psalm 19:

> *The heavens declare the glory of God,*
>   *and the firmament tells His handiwork.*
> *Day unto day utters the tale,*
>   *night unto night unfolds knowledge.*
> *There is no word, no speech,*
>   *their voice is not heard,*
> *yet their course extends through all the earth,*
>   *and their theme to the end of the world.*

God is manifest in the world He created. The natural rhythms and natural phenomena are reflections of the greatness of the Creator. Jewish spirituality is intimately linked to the natural world, and through the natural world to God. Nature is filled with suggestions, symbols, invitations. The religious person is sensitive to these messages and responds to them with blessings and special observances.

The Torah and the universe have the same Author.

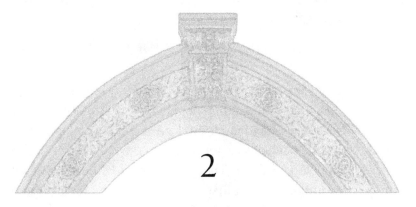

2

THE LIMITATIONS OF SYSTEMATIC THEOLOGY

Jewish religious experience, as has been seen, is intimately linked to the rhythms of the natural world. The rhythms of the sun and moon govern our times of prayer, our religious festivals, our meditation on the universe. The phenomena of nature evoke within us responses to the greatness of God the Creator and we recite blessings on witnessing the powers of nature.

Centuries of Westernization and urbanization have profoundly affected Jewish religious sensitivity. There has been a steady and increasing alienation between Jewish religious observance and the natural world, with a parallel diminution in sensing awe for God as Creator of the natural universe.

To illustrate this changed perception, we may consider the commonly observed Jewish religious experiences that recur on a regular basis. Modern Jews identify their religious lives with such events as the Passover seder, the High Holy Days synagogue services, the Friday night Shabbat ceremonies and meal, the study of Torah, and synagogue worship. A common denominator of these observances is that they generally happen *indoors*. They are observances in a synagogue, a home, or a place of study.

If we were to consider the situation of the ancient Israelites, we would be confronted with a different religious sensibility. The most important observances for them would have included the three pilgrimages to Jerusalem when they journeyed to the holy city to celebrate Passover, Shavuot, and Sukkot. They would include the observance of Bikkurim, the bringing of the first fruits to the Temple, a ceremony that was a great outdoor celebration. They would include the festivities that took place during the harvest festivals, the sharing of harvests with the poor, the bringing of animals to Jerusalem to be offered as sacrifices. Almost everything, in fact, would have involved being *outdoors*, in contact with the natural world.

Obviously, we have moved a long way from the agricultural life of ancient Israel to the urban life of contemporary society. Our religious images and observances, the things we consider essential and meaningful, have been transformed over the generations due to sociological and demographic changes. By urbanizing religion and by placing its most important events indoors, we have lost touch with the original religious insight that connected us with the rhythms of nature.

Jewish law often speaks in the old, natural language. We have seen in the previous chapter how dependent religious life was on the natural order of the universe. But today when we discuss the times of prayer, we speak not of sunrise or sunset so much as of specific times such as 7 a.m. or 6 p.m. In former times, Jews knew when the Sabbath was concluded by going outside and looking for stars. If it was dark enough to be able to observe three stars, then the Sabbath was over. Today, calendars and synagogue schedules list the time when Sabbath ends with the arrogant precision of mathematics. A person may pray in the morning without having experienced sunrise; she may pray in the afternoon without having experienced sunset; she may say evening prayers without having seen a star in the sky. Religious life can be celebrated indoors with the assistance of clocks and calendars, without the need arising to go outside and determine the position of the sun.

By bringing religion indoors, some of our feeling of awe for the universe and its Creator has been lost. The regular daily connections with nature that Jewish tradition has prescribed are no longer easily experienced. But losing contact with the natural world threatens to make religion increasingly artificial, removed from its basic life source.

The Jewish ideal of a religious person has undergone a change over the centuries. Until relatively modern times, the ideal religious personality was one who spent much time outdoors, who contemplated the wonders of the universe and the wisdom of its Maker. The ideal Jew lived in harmony with nature and participated in its rhythms. The notion that ideal piety can be found in a pale, scholarly, undernourished saint who spends his days and nights studying Torah in a study hall is not true to the original Jewish religious vision. The biblical heroes and prophets, the Talmudic sages, the medieval pietists and mystics—all were involved in outdoor religion.

Prayer and Windows

Attitudes about spirituality are suggested by the kind of windows used in places of worship. Windows are the connection between the indoor world and the world outside. The location and transparency of the windows indicate the extent to which worshippers are expected to relate to the world outdoors while they are engaged in prayer.

The Talmud records the opinion of Rabbi Hiyya bar Abba in the name of Rabbi Yohanan: "A person should not pray except in a house which has windows" (*Berakhot* 34b). The proof text is drawn from the book of Daniel. Since Daniel offered his prayers while looking through a window in the direction of Jerusalem, so this precedent should be followed by subsequent generations. The commentator Rabbi Shlomo Yitzhaki (Rashi) explains that "windows cause one to concentrate his heart, since he looks toward the heavens and his heart is humbled." According to this opinion, a person praying indoors may reach a higher spiritual level by looking out a window to see the heavens.

Yet windows in synagogues have varied from place to place and generation to generation, reflecting different attitudes toward the outside world. In some synagogues, windows were built high up on the wall, above the height of any person. This was done in order to prevent people from being distracted from their prayers by letting their eyes wander to the outdoors during services. Windows, which serve to bring the outside in, also serve to connect the inside with the outside. If praying requires concentration on the words of the prayer, windows can be distracting. Indeed, a fear of the distraction of windows emerged in many communities. Windows, even when placed high up on the synagogue walls, were considered a necessary evil at worst, or at best a possible aid to prayer only in the event that one was unable to concentrate properly on one's own. The commentary *Magen Avraham* on the *Shulhan Arukh* states that one's eyes should be directed downward during prayer. "Nevertheless, when one's concentration is broken, one can lift the eyes toward the heavens in order to awaken concentration" (commentary on *Orah Hayyim* 90:4).

The fear of windows is evident in a feature common to almost all Western synagogues: stained glass. The use of stained-glass windows has a long history in Christian Europe, with great churches boasting artistic windows, some quite ancient. Apparently European Jews were impressed by this feature of Christian religious architecture, so synagogues began to have stained-glass windows too.

Stained-glass windows, though they may be very beautiful, were not incorporated into religious architecture merely for the sake of beauty. The desire for artistic beauty could have been satisfied by tapestries, frescoes, wall carvings, etc. Although generations of cultural conditioning have made us accustomed to stained-glass windows in houses of worship, there is no intrinsic need for them from an aesthetic point of view. The windows reflect a philosophical attitude on prayer and our sense of spirituality.

Normally windows exist to let the outside world enter the world indoors. Stained-glass windows, however, serve the opposite function: they keep the outside world outside. They protect the indoor world from intrusions from the outside.

Stained-glass windows create an artificial world of indoor spirituality. Upon entering a synagogue with stained-glass windows, for example, we enter a religious realm, a world unto itself without reference to anything outside. It is irrelevant where such a synagogue is actually located: it might be in the middle of New York City or in China or on top of a mountain or along a seashore. To a person inside the synagogue, the outside world is closed out; it cannot penetrate the colored windows.

The underlying motivation for creating such windows is the belief, whether acknowledged or not, that prayer can best be experienced in a place that is closed off from the distractions of the outside world. When one enters a synagogue with stained-glass windows, one knows immediately that this is a place of worship. The inwardness of the building makes its message known.

But there have been many synagogues where the windows have been clear, where worshippers could see what was going on outside. In such synagogues, people could recite their prayers while also viewing gardens, trees, and other outdoor scenery. The synagogue of Rabbi Yosef Karo in Safed, for example, has clear windows through which one can see the wonderful mountainous scenery of the Galilee. Synagogues with clear windows reflect no fear of the outside world, no need to create an artificially enclosed structure for prayer to God.

Since the natural world and the spiritual world are organically connected, the Talmudic requirement of praying only in a house with windows makes much sense. But the windows should be clear; they should be an opening between the person praying and God, Creator of heaven and earth. Stained-glass windows symbolize a changed sense of spirituality, a break from traditional outdoor religiosity.

The windows in our houses of worship are also windows to our souls. They represent our attitudes toward the outside world, and toward the inside world, and toward the world inside each of us.

Natural Experience Versus Intellectual Abstraction

From infancy, we are taught what to ignore and what to notice. Our sensory organs receive numerous stimuli constantly, so we are trained to focus on specific stimuli rather than to deal with everything at once. Our eyes focus on details; our ears listen for specific sounds and voices.

We pay no attention to so many things that occur to us because we are trained to ignore them. Do you feel your heart beating? Do you feel the pressure of your feet as they rest on the ground? Do you see, hear, smell, feel, or taste all the stimuli which assault you at this moment? No. It would be annoying if we could not control our sensory powers to some extent in order to diminish the impact of stimuli on us when we neither want nor need them.

There are different ways of perceiving reality. Our senses are trained by our upbringing to relay what is considered important and to put aside things that are considered extraneous. For example, the Western mind focuses on objects, on solid forms, on individual people. The Eastern mind tends to absorb objects, solid forms, and individual people in their relationship with space and with everything else around them.

We are not, therefore, objective in our description of reality. To a large extent, we see and describe reality in the way our culture has taught us to do.[1] This observation relates not only to our sensory perceptions but also to our ways of viewing history, religion, and civilization. We tend to think in patterns that we have inherited without realizing how our understanding is limited and biased.

For example, Western civilization places significant emphasis on intellectuality and analytical thinking. Greek philosophy has set the pattern for searching for truth, for scientific investigation, and for logical reasoning. Western tradition stresses systematic philosophy, with its orderliness and abundance of proofs.

Western philosophical works, including works by Jewish thinkers, have been concerned with such questions as the existence of God, epistemology, and ultimate Truth. Western thinkers have developed systematic theology, with axioms, proofs, and logical demonstrations. Psychology and psychiatry have also developed in the West, reflecting this civilization's desire to understand everything in an analytic, scientific fashion. Even our own minds and thoughts are subjected to the process of analysis.

Through centuries of Western influence, the discourses of Jewish philosophy have adopted Western analytic methods. Jewish thinkers—such as Philo, Saadiah, and Maimonides, to name only several—have attempted to present Judaism in a systematic and reasonable way. Jewish philosophers delineated principles of the Jewish faith, elaborating on their meanings and implications. They suggested a rational basis for the commandments of the Torah. Yet these features of Western philosophy were not indigenous to Jewish thought. Rather, they were adopted due to outside influence.

Moses and Aristotle represent very different world views. Moses spoke to God face-to-face. He did not need to prove the existence of God or to provide any philosophical arguments for God's reality. Aristotle, on the other hand, devised logical proofs to demonstrate a first cause, an unmoved mover. Moses experienced God as a living reality; Aristotle could not imagine speaking to God face-to-face. Whereas Greek philosophers engaged in philosophical speculation to find truth, biblical characters and prophets conversed with God—the ultimate source of truth—quite naturally and calmly, as though it was a perfectly normal circumstance to communicate with Him.

Western philosophy has difficulty understanding the biblical world view. It can deal with proofs and systems, but it cannot deal seriously with spontaneous experiences, with revelations from God, with mystical insights. In order to understand the Jewish worldview on its own terms, we need to transcend the intellectual constraints imposed on our thinking by Western philosophy.

The Torah presents no philosophical arguments, no theological discourses. It speaks in its own idiom, with its own assumptions. Moses saw no need to present a systematic list of principles of faith. Jews lived for millennia without systematic philosophy and apparently felt no lack in their religious lives due to this absence. The tradition of the Torah is a tradition of direct, holistic relationship with God. The tradition flows with the natural rhythms of the universe. The original truths of the Torah are in the domain of experience rather than speculation. The Torah is remarkably non-theological and non-philosophical, being primarily concerned with describing people in their relationships with each other and with God. Its concern is life rather than abstract thought.

Words of the Torah

Words are symbols that we use in order to communicate with each other. Words are not reality; they simply suggest a reality. For example, we may all agree to call a flat board resting on four legs a table. But this object is not a table, only something that we agree to call a table. It is actually a combination of atoms, energy, and matter; it is, in fact, so complicated that it would be nearly impossible to describe everything about it. We simplify such a thing by calling it a table, and we all understand what we are talking about. When we use words that symbolize emotions, the words are approximations of feelings, not the feelings themselves. Our words are used as suggestions, analogies, intimations. No one can fully express feelings or ideas, since something is lost in transforming these feelings and ideas into words, or into other symbols such as art or music.

This dilemma was expressed by the famous sixteenth-century mystic Rabbi Yizhak Luria, who lived in Safed. One of his students asked him why he did not write his teachings down in books. Rabbi Luria answered: "It is impossible, because all things are interrelated. I can hardly open my mouth to speak without feeling as though the sea burst its dams and overflowed. How then shall I express what my soul has received, and how can I put it down in a book?" Experience and understanding are too vast; words are too inadequate.[2]

The word that is perhaps the ultimate symbol is "God." This word evokes deep feelings and ideas. Since it is impossible for us to express ourselves completely, we limit ourselves by using a word: God. When we say that God is just, or that God is merciful, we are using symbolic, suggestive language. These words are reflections of feelings we have (or would like to have) about the force that we call God. But no attribute of God is anything more than a suggestion or a wish, and no word truly expresses reality but only suggests reality.

The Torah, of course, is composed of words. God revealed Himself to the Israelites through words. He created the world through words. Yet these words too—though divine in origin—are suggestive and symbolic. Rabbi Ishmael, one of the outstanding Talmudic sages, taught that the Torah speaks in the language of humans (*Sanhedrin* 64b). God conveyed something about God's self by means of words, symbols that could be meaningful to humans.

A midrash relates that when God was preparing to give the Torah to the people of Israel, the angels in heaven argued that they themselves should be given the Torah, not the Israelites. God called Moses to heaven to answer the claim of the angels. Moses told the angels quite simply that the Torah was not relevant to them. Did they leave Egypt? Did they have jealousies so that they needed special commandments governing their behavior? Did they have parents to honor? In short, the text of the Torah related to Israel, not to angels. God was pleased with Moses' refutation of the angels' claim and therefore did give the Torah to Israel.

Rabbi Yosef Hayyim of Baghdad (late nineteenth to early twentieth century) was bothered by this midrash.[3] Didn't the angels know what was written in the Torah? Why did they make their claim in the first place? They should have realized that it was not relevant to them but only to the Israelites. Rabbi Yosef Hayyim resolved this difficulty with the following explanation: The words of the Torah have two levels of meaning—the *peshat,* the simple external meaning; and the *sod,* the hidden deeper meaning. The *peshat* indeed is not relevant to angels, but the *sod* is, and it was for the *sod* that they argued. The angels ignored the literal meaning of the words, seeing only their profound truths.

Rabbi Moshe ben Nahman, one of the great medieval Sephardic mystics and commentators, notes in the preface to his commentary on the Torah:

> We possess an authentic tradition showing that the entire Torah consists of the names of God, and that the words we read can be divided in a different way so as to form [God's] names.... The statement in the Aggadah that the Torah was originally written with black fire on white fire confirms our belief that the writing was continuous, without divisions into words, which made it possible for the Torah to be read either as a sequence of [God's] names or in the traditional way as history and commandments.

> The Torah as given to Moses was divided into words in such
> a way as to be read as divine commandments. But at the same
> time, he received the oral tradition, whereby it was to be read as
> a sequence of names.

The words of the Torah are suggestions of deeper truths. A rabbinic
legend had it that Rabbi Akiva was not only able to understand the
meaning of each word and letter of the Torah, but he also could interpret the ornamental crowns (*taggin*) that grace some of the letters of the
Torah scroll. Since the Torah is a revealed text of God, its words, and
even its ornamental crowns, are of profound significance.

When we attempt to understand the Torah and authentic Jewish
spirituality, we need to be mindful of the strong cultural biases we
have inherited from the Western philosophical tradition. The urbanization and Westernization of the past centuries have moved us away
from central religious insights of the Torah tradition. As we open our
eyes more to the outdoors, to the rhythms of nature, we will come
into relationship with God, Creator of the universe. The Torah and its
words are guides to experience, symbols of undefined and undefin-
able truths. Jewish spirituality entails appreciating the value of calm,
natural wisdom and being aware of the limitations of abstract, analytic,
systematic philosophy.

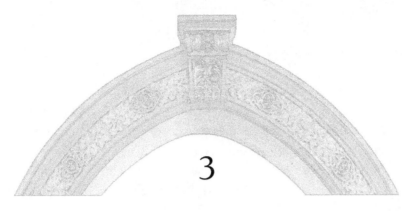

3

THE RHYTHMS
OF TIME

Sacred Time

Mircea Eliade has observed in his book *The Sacred and the Profane* that human beings experience time on two levels. First and most obvious is normal time, the time contemporary with our lives. This kind of time is linear. It has a beginning—our birth; a middle—the years of our life; and an end—our death. But there is also another kind of time that we experience but that is not contemporary with our lives. This is sacred time, time contemporary with an original sacred event, the time of Creation, the time of the "myths of the gods."

Eliade writes: "Hence religious man lives in two kinds of time, of which the most important, sacred time, appears under the paradoxical aspect of circular time, reversible and recoverable, a sort of eternal mythical present that is periodically reintegrated by means of rites."[1] Thus, a religious person does not live only in the historical present. She also experiences a return to a sacred time as it occurred *ab origine* (in the beginning), in *illo tempore* (at that time). The ceremonies of religious festivals serve the purpose of leading the religious person into that original sacred time.

Eliade has written that "the participants in the festival become contemporaries of the mythical event."

In other words, they emerge from their historical time ... and recover primordial time, which is always the same, which belongs to eternity. Religious man periodically finds his way into mythical and sacred time, re-enters the time of origin, the time that 'floweth not' because it does not participate in profane temporal duration, because it is composed of an eternal present, which is indefinitely recoverable.[2]

A religious person enters this sacred and indestructible time. The yearly calendar includes the same sacred festivals, commemorating the same mythical events. Each year, the religious person has the possibility of experiencing periodic returns to primordial situations by entering sacred time. For religious people of the primitive and archaic societies, "it is by virtue of this eternal return to the sources of the sacred and the real that human existence appears to be saved from nothingness and death."[3]

Eliade observes that Judaism offered a major innovation over the archaic religions and over the ideal of eternal return as elaborated in India and Greece. "For Judaism, time has a beginning and will have an end. The idea of cyclic time is left behind."[4] In other words, Judaism perceives time as being linear rather than cyclical. Sacred events are part of normal human history. In commemorating these events, the religious Jew does not re-enter the original sacred time, but only experiences it as a historical memory.

Although Eliade's description of Judaism's innovation is essentially valid, it must be said that Jews also experience sacred time that involves a return to origins. Time is indeed linear; yet historic flashbacks bring the religious Jew to feel as though he experienced the primal religious events. In fact, Jewish ritual's genius is in its demand to involve Jews in a symbolic reliving of past events, not just intellectually recounting them as historical phenomena. A consideration of the Jewish festivals and religious commemorations will clarify the Jewish experience of sacred time.

High Holy Days

The Torah refers to the first day of the seventh month as a day of sounding the shofar (ram's horn). The tenth day of the seventh month is designated as a day of atonement.

Jewish tradition has highlighted these days so that they have come to be known popularly as the High Holy Days or the Days of Awe (*Yamim Nora'im*). The first day of the month is Rosh Hashanah (the New Year) while the tenth day of the month is the fast day of Yom Kippur. Rosh Hashanah is generally observed in commemoration of God's creation of the world.[5]

The season of the High Holy Days is characterized by the belief that God stands in judgment of each of us during this period. God decides who will live and who will die, who will prosper and who will not, who will be healthy and who will be ill. The holidays are preceded by a month of *selihot* (penitential prayers), when Jews ask for forgiveness for their sins and assure God that they will do better during the coming year. Rosh Hashanah and Yom Kippur are solemn days of introspection, self-criticism, and meditation on the meaning of one's life.

These themes are common to other ancient religions. Eliade has written that the New Year was observed among ancient religions as a restoration of primordial time, the pure time that existed at the moment of creation:

> This is why the New Year is the occasion for "purifications," for the expulsion of sins, of demons, or merely of a scapegoat. For it is not a matter merely of a certain temporal interval coming to its end and the beginning of another (as a modern man, for example, thinks); it is also a matter of abolishing the past year and past time. Indeed, this is the meaning of ritual purification; there is more than a mere "purification;" the sins and faults of the individual and of the community as a whole are annulled, *consumed as by fire.*[6]

Yet the Jewish observance of the New Year does not intend to transfer the religious Jew to the primordial time of Creation. Indeed, the early sages of Israel gave very little emphasis to the theme of God's creation of the universe on the New Year. Interestingly, the Torah reading in the synagogue on Rosh Hashanah deals with Abraham's expulsion of Ishmael and his binding of Isaac. It does not recount the Creation story that opens the Torah in Genesis. The New Year is surely a time to reflect about God as Creator of the universe; but even more importantly, it is a time to reflect on the meaning of life, the degree of our own faith and religious commitment, and our connection to the people of Israel, going back to our founding couple, Abraham and Sarah. Although the Jewish New Year does have some of the elements of the New Year as observed by ancient religions with cyclical time, the Jewish High Holy Days do not involve a return to the original sacred time of Creation.

The Pilgrim Festivals

The three biblical pilgrim festivals were originally connected to the harvest celebrations. But they were also associated with historical religious events.

Sukkot

Sukkot commemorates the fact that the Israelites dwelled in temporary booths (*sukkah*) during their forty years of wandering in the wilderness. They survived this ordeal only through God's merciful providence. Sukkot is observed not by giving a historical lecture on the Israelites' wanderings, but by the actual construction of booths in which to dwell for the duration of the holiday. According to Jewish law, the booths may not have closed roofs but should be covered by loose branches or greens. During the festival, Jews are supposed to consider the *sukkah* as their regular home and spend as much time as possible in it. One should eat all meals in the *sukkah*. In warm climates it has been customary for people to sleep in the *sukkah* as well. These laws are definite attempts to make Jews vicariously experience the wanderings of the ancient Israelites. We literally live in the same kind of temporary booths as our ancestors did; we want to experience in some measure what they experienced. Our observance makes us—at least in some way—contemporaries of the Israelites who experienced the original sacred time that gives meaning to this festival. Although the Jewish sense of time is linear, we have in this festival an example of a spiritual flashback where we try to relive and recapture the experience of our ancestors.

Pesah

Pesah (Passover) celebrates the miraculous exodus of the Israelites from the slavery of Egypt. The Torah recounts how God appointed Moses and Aaron to represent the Israelites before Pharaoh. Pharaoh refused to free the Israelites, so the Egyptians suffered ten plagues, culminating with the death of the firstborn. The Israelites were spared from the ravages of these plagues. Finally, Pharaoh allowed the slaves to leave and the exodus began.

Once the Israelites had left, however, Pharaoh had a change of heart and sent his warriors after them. The Red Sea split before Moses and his people and all of them crossed safely to the other side. The Egyptians who pursued them were drowned as the sea came back together once the Israelites had passed through.

The festival of Pesah is observed by reliving vicariously the experiences of the ancient Israelites. For the duration of the holiday, Jews eat matzah (unleavened bread) rather than regular leavened bread. This is a reminder that the Israelites had no time to bake bread in their haste to leave slavery. Moreover, the matzah is symbolic of the bread of affliction that our ancestors ate while they were slaves.

On the first night of Pesah—or on the first two nights, in the diaspora—a special home service is held known as a seder. Aside from eating matzah, bitter herbs are also eaten to recall the bitter times suffered by our ancestors. Many Sephardic Jews have the custom of placing a piece of matzah in a sack and carrying it on their shoulders as though they were among the Israelites of old carrying their belongings as they escaped from Egypt. The main text of the seder is the Haggadah, which recounts the exodus from Egypt and the great wonders performed by God on behalf of the people of Israel. The Haggadah states that in each generation Jews are to feel as though they themselves participated in the exodus from Egypt. In other words, there is a clear attempt to recapture an ancient sacred time by reliving it in thought, symbol, and vicarious experience.

Ostensibly Pesah is a celebration of a historic event. Yet it is not really history that makes this festival meaningful. On the contrary, the dominating feature is a national memory of an ancient event that is important not as a historical fact, but as a spiritual and emotional framework for our religious life.

That our main concern on Pesah is not pure history should be fairly obvious. In our recounting the story of the exodus, we do not provide a learned dissertation drawing on historical and archaeological sources. A great many details are omitted. The biblical story itself is not presented in the style of historical scholarship. If our main concern on this festival is to recount history, then the Haggadah should read like a history text. It doesn't.

Professor Yosef Hayim Yerushalmi, in his book *Zakhor: Jewish History and Jewish Memory*, has noted that historiography in the modern sense is something different from memory. Actually, it challenges memory. It discovers new facts and creates new perceptions. When we recount the story of the exodus of the Israelites, we are not engaging in the work of historians. Rather, we are sharing a historical national memory and we are attempting to identify ourselves with our redeemed ancestors.

Yerushalmi points out a paradox. In the modern era, we have made incredible advances in uncovering the past and in advancing historical research. Yet at the same time our sense of continuity with the past has steadily declined. Hans Meyerhoff has noted: "Previous generations knew much less about the past than we do, but perhaps *felt* a much greater sense of identity and continuity with it."[7] Jews existed for millennia without scientific historians. Collective national memory provided continuity for all Jews in all places at all times. In blessing God in the Haggadah, we state that God has "redeemed us and redeemed our ancestors." We connect ourselves with those who have come before us. We have, in a sense, seen ourselves as being contemporaries of our ancestors. Put in other terms, the festival is an opportunity to experience sacred time. This experience is not provided by the intellect and reason; it is provided by national memory, by emotion and imagination, by a sense of continuity with family and ancestors.

Aside from the seder observances, other Pesah customs place us in a kind of sacred time. The Torah reading for the seventh day of Pesah is the description of the crossing of the Red Sea, and includes the moving song that Moses and the people of Israel sang upon their redemption. Also, on the night on which the festival concludes, it is customary among some Sephardic communities for parents and grandparents to return home from the synagogue while their children and grandchildren eagerly await them. With great joy, with singing and gladness, the parents and grandparents open the door to the home, and throw handfuls of coins, candy, and grass, and all the children scramble to collect the treasures. The custom harks back to the joy the Israelites experienced upon crossing the Red Sea. The coins are reminders of the fact that the Egyptians gave the Israelites gold and silver before the exodus began. The grass recalls the reeds along the Red Sea. The candy, which is generally a symbol of sweetness and happiness, may also call to mind the manna that God provided to the Israelites after they crossed the Red Sea.

These customs and observances help us to transcend the present time in order to participate in a sacred time. While never losing awareness of the present, we also share the emotions, feelings, and thoughts of our ancestors in their original relationship with God.

Shavuot

The festival of Shavuot, which occurs seven weeks after the second night of Pesah, was originally celebrated as a harvest festival. It has the added historical association of being the time when God revealed the Ten Commandments to the children of Israel at Mount Sinai. The festival is only one day in Israel, but two days in the diaspora. Many religious Jews stay up all night on the evening of Shavuot in order to study Torah. This custom is a symbolic gesture in which Jews demonstrate their total love and commitment to the Torah, God's revealed word. Interestingly, it was at one of these all-night study vigils on the eve of Shavuot that the famous sixteenth-century scholar and mystic Rabbi Yosef Karo received a personal divine revelation through a *maggid*, an angelic voice.

On the morning of Shavuot, the Torah reading in the synagogue is the section of Exodus describing the revelation at Sinai. The prophetic portion is the beginning of the book of Ezekiel, in which the prophet describes his vision of God on His throne of glory. The intention of these readings is to draw us into the experience of revelation.

Commemorations

The Jewish calendar includes a number of days that commemorate ancient happenings. In each case, Jews are expected to participate in sacred time, not merely to understand intellectually the details that are the reason for the commemoration.

Hanukkah

The holiday of Hanukkah celebrates the victory of the Maccabees over the Hellenistic Syrians in the second century BCE. Tradition has it that when the Maccabees regained control of the Temple in Jerusalem, they wished to light the menorah—the seven-branched candelabra of the Temple. But they found only one jar of pure oil with enough fuel to last one day. Miraculously, it lasted eight days, giving the people enough time to make new pure oil. In celebration of Hanukkah, Jews are obligated to light a menorah in their homes on each of the eight nights of the festival. The lights are to be lit near a window so that people walking in the street can see them and be aware of the wonderful miracle that occurred to the Jewish people. A special paragraph is added in the silent devotion of the three daily prayers, as well as in the Grace after Meals, in which God is praised for having given victory to the small, valiant Israelite army that faced such a formidable foe.

The significance of this festival is not in the precise historical details of the Maccabean revolution, but rather in the emotional, nationalistic memories. The holiday has always been a source of encouragement to Jews who have faced enemies of great strength and number. The Maccabees proved that a small faithful group of Jews could defeat seemingly more powerful enemies. The lighting of the Hanukkah candles is a yearly reminder of God's providence over Israel and of Israel's devotion to its religious freedom and national identity.

Purim

The festival of Purim celebrates the salvation of the ancient Persian Jewish community through the leadership of Mordecai and Esther.

The king's advisor Haman received the king's approval for a plan to destroy all the Jews in his kingdom. Instead, the Jews were saved and Haman himself was hanged. To celebrate this day, Jews read the scroll of Esther, the vivid biblical narrative recounting the Purim story. One of the obligations of the day is to have a festive meal in order to enjoy the happiness of the day. It is also incumbent upon Jews to give charity to the poor and to send gifts of food to friends and neighbors on Purim. These obligations teach the importance of sharing and caring for others. They create goodwill in the community. Purim thus becomes not merely a day for remembering an ancient redemption of Jews, but also a day for joy and happiness within contemporary Jewish communities.

The Ninth of Av

The Jewish calendar includes a number of fast days commemorating sad events that occurred to the Jewish people in the past. The most dramatic of these fast days is the ninth of the month of Av. This day is traditionally associated with the destruction of both the First and Second Temples in Jerusalem. Following the destruction of the Second Temple by the Romans in 70 CE, the Jews lived in exile for nearly nineteen hundred years before regaining sovereignty in the land of Israel.

The ninth of Av is observed by fasting the complete day, from before sunset on the eve of the ninth until after sunset on the ninth. Customs of mourning are kept, such as wearing non-leather shoes, sitting on the floor, and avoiding social conversation. The prayer services are characterized by melancholy melodies, the chanting of dirges and laments. The day closes with a note of consolation, with readings from the prophet Isaiah in which God promises to restore Israel to its former glory. As with the other sacred times discussed earlier, the purpose of this day is not to gain academic knowledge about historical events, but rather to share the sacred time in which those events occurred. The key to understanding these holidays and commemorations is in the realm of experience, emotion, memory; not in reason, scientific research, or over-intellectualization.

Sabbath

The holiest of Jewish holy days is Shabbat, the Sabbath. It begins at sunset on Friday evening and ends after sundown on Saturday night.

The holiness of Shabbat is not observable objectively. Unlike Rosh Hodesh or the seasonal festivals, there is no clear pattern in the natural world that would indicate that the seventh day of every week should be considered sacred. There is no scientifically observable difference between time on the Sabbath and time on any other day of the week. The day is sacred and noteworthy only to those who are spiritually attuned to its sanctity. Shabbat is a commemoration of God as Creator. The Torah opens with the account of Creation in which God created the world in six stages, and during the seventh stage He rested. Likewise, we symbolically acknowledge this process of creation by working on six days and resting on the seventh. Thus Shabbat becomes an expression of our recognition of the original rhythm of God's act of creation.

The intentional desecration of Shabbat is considered by the Torah to be a capital offense. The Talmud and Jewish law consider one who has willfully violated the Sabbath to be in the same category as one who has worshipped idols. By desecrating Shabbat, a person denies that God created the universe and that God Himself sanctified the seventh day as Shabbat. Since this concept is so fundamental to Jewish belief, one who discards it intentionally has separated herself from the people of Israel and the God of Israel.

On Shabbat, one is obliged to abstain from thirty-nine types of creative activity, such as building, plowing, writing, or sewing. These endeavors reflect human control of nature. For six days of each week, we are empowered to mold the natural world to meet our needs—to build, to plow, to cut and shape. We light fires; we transport merchandise. On Shabbat, though, we abstain from these weekday activities. We recognize, not just by philosophical meditation but by symbolic emulation, that God is the sole Creator and Master of the universe. On the seventh day, when we are not engaged in controlling the natural world, the natural world continues to be sustained by God's power.

It is a lesson in humility for humans to realize that they are not the ultimate controllers of the natural world.

But Shabbat is not merely a day to abstain from certain kinds of activity. It is also a day for the positive experience of joy, family togetherness, and communal interrelatedness. Shabbat is sanctified in the home with the lighting of candles before sunset, the eating of three festive meals during Shabbat, the singing of hymns around the family table. Shabbat is also sanctified in the prayer services, Torah study, and reaffirmation of friendships that take place in synagogue.

Jewish law and custom prescribe that Shabbat must be respected by wearing nice clothes, by preparing special foods, by studying Torah, and by participating in communal prayer. By changing our accustomed ways, we leave profane time and enter the sacred time of Shabbat.

Rabbi Elazar Azikri, a sixteenth-century Sephardic mystic, has explained in his book *Sefer Hareidim* that the three meals eaten in honor of Shabbat relate to the three major themes of the day.[8] The Friday night meal relates to the Shabbat of Creation, when God had completed the work of creating the universe in six days and then sanctified the seventh day. The blessing over wine on Friday evening that precedes the Shabbat meal is introduced with the chanting of the biblical verses describing that first Shabbat of Creation. The meal of Shabbat morning is connected to the Shabbat laws as revealed to the children of Israel on Mount Sinai. The morning prayer makes reference to the fact that Shabbat was given as a commandment to the children of Israel by God at Sinai. The Shabbat afternoon meal is related to the world that is all Shabbat, the future messianic period. This theme, too, is central to the afternoon prayer that refers to God as being One and His name One, an allusion to messianic times when everyone will recognize the true One God.

Kabbalists have attached great importance to yet a fourth meal, one that is served after Shabbat has already ended. This is known as the *Melaveh Malkah,* the escorting of the Shabbat Queen. Just as the Shabbat Queen is welcomed on Friday evening with the *Lekha Dodi* hymn, so she is to be properly escorted on her departure.

At the conclusion of Shabbat, a special ceremony known as *Havdalah* (separation) symbolizes the return to non-sacred time. A blessing is recited over wine and over the fragrance of spices, herbs, or fruit. Then a blessing is made over the light of a candle with several wicks, indicating that we may once again create fire and return to the regular tasks of the six work days. The *Havdalah* concludes with a blessing praising God for having separated between the holy and the profane, between light and darkness, between Israel and the nations, and between the Shabbat and the six work days. The sacred time of Shabbat, then, is set off at the beginning with the lights of the Shabbat candles and at the end with the fire of *Havdalah*. The time between these fires is categorically different from the profane time of the rest of the week. But no one can experience that sacred time unless he or she enters it consciously and with spiritual awareness.

In considering the sacred times of the Jewish people, we have seen that they involve a vicarious experience of primordial religious events. The symbols of the festivals and the Sabbath bring us back to the time of the creation of the world and to the major events of the ancient Israelites— exodus and revelation. Jewish traditions lead us to reminisce about those original events, even to feel as though we were somehow part of them. Yet even in the midst of experiencing sacred time, the religious Jew does not surrender completely to those ancient events. Judaism does not let us lose consciousness of the present time, the linear time that runs from creation through history and to ultimate redemption. We may experience vicariously the original religious events, but we must always realize that we cannot actually return to them; time is not cyclical. We remember the past, we participate in it through symbol and thought. But we remain distinctly in the here and now, fully conscious of the unfolding of history.

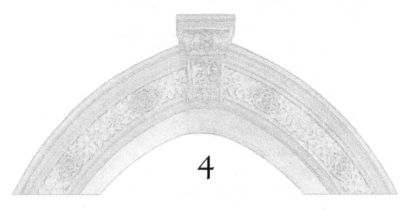

4

SACRED PLACES

Paradox and Terror

The Western mind has been troubled by the fact that humans are paradoxical beings. On the one hand, we are part of the natural world. Our
bodies function like those of other animals: we go through the process
of birth, life, decay, and death. On the other hand, human beings have
a symbolic identity that lifts us sharply out of nature. Ernest Becker,
in his thoughtful volume *The Denial of Death,* has argued that a person

> is a symbolic self, a creature with a name, a life history. He is
> a creator with a mind that soars out to speculate about atoms
> and infinity, who can place himself imaginatively at a point in
> space and contemplate bemusedly his own planet. This immense
> expansion, this dexterity, this ethereality, this self-consciousness
> gives to man literally the status of a small god in nature, as the
> Renaissance thinkers knew.[1]

Becker has called this existential paradox the condition of "individuality within finitude." He has contended that in recent times every
psychologist who has done vital work has made this paradox the main
problem of his thought.

The result of this existential paradox, according to Becker, is terror.

> Man is literally split in two: he has an awareness of his splendid
> uniqueness in that he sticks out of nature with a towering majesty,

and yet he goes back into the ground a few feet in order blindly
and dumbly to rot and disappear forever. It is a terrifying dilemma
to be in and to have to live with.[2]

Lower animals are spared from this paradox, since they lack self-
consciousness and anxiety about death. They simply live day by day
as natural organisms. But since humans have a mind that can think
abstractly, that gives one a sense of personal identity, the prospect of
being limited by a body and of dying creates dread.

Perhaps the terror to which Becker refers does not stem from the
consciousness of death per se. Rather, it may derive from a person's
feeling of meaninglessness. If one feels that life has no value, no ultimate meaning, then death indeed can seem frightening. If life has no
meaning, death becomes a meaningless end to a meaningless existence.
Since Western society stresses individuality, fame, success, etc., death
becomes a nasty obstacle that prevents us from continuing to gain
fame, wealth, power. And if life has no transcendent meaning, then
death is ugly and terrifying.

Jewish tradition has not been overly concerned with the dualism
and terror posited by Becker and others. To be sure, there has long
been an awareness of the existential paradox of human life. In Psalm
8, the psalmist has expressed the problem.

> When I look up at Your heavens, the work of Your fingers,
>   the moon and the stars set in their places by You—
> what is man that You should be mindful of him,
>   a mortal being that You should care for him?
> Yet You have made him a little lower than angels,
>   crowning him with glory and honor.

The dilemma is an integral part of human existence. Yet, the religious
person need feel no terror or anxiety because of it. One can live with
paradox and still remain calm.

What is a human's place in the eternity of time and the vastness of
space? The span of human life is infinitesimal compared to eternity.

Our greatest achievements are ultimately insignificant and transient. Even if our fame can last for a thousand years or ten thousand years, what is that compared to the endlessness of time? The Jewish prayer book expresses this truth in a passage read very early in the morning service:

> *What are we? What is our life? What our goodness? What our righteousness?*
> *What our help? What our strength? What our power?*
> *What can we say in Your presence, Lord our God, God of our ancestors?*
> *Are not the mightiest as naught before You, people of renown as if they were not, the wise as if without knowledge, the intelligent as if lacking in understanding?*
> *For our doings are often confusion, and the days of our life as vanity before You.*

Jewish religious tradition deals with this dilemma in several ways. We have seen in the first chapter that Jewish spirituality is linked to the rhythms of nature. The natural world is an expression of God the Creator. Even if we are awed by the vastness of nature and the greatness of God, we are also drawn closer to nature and to God. The alienation and fear give way to humility and love.

To speculate about the meaning of our lives in the face of eternity is depressing—and useless. Religious tradition attempts to keep alive our sense of wonder while at the same time making us feel more comfortable with existential reality. Since we have the possibility of experiencing a spiritual relationship with the eternal God, life does have meaning; spiritual fulfillment can be attained.

Sacred time gives us the possibility of sharing eternity, of bringing time into humanly comprehensible terms. And since the universe is so vast that a person might feel like an atom in an endless physical cosmos, religion has the concept of sacred space. By designating particular places as being sacred, the religious person can live within her allotted space with meaning and dignity.

Sacred Space

The Torah records the dream of Jacob in which he saw a ladder connecting heaven and earth, with angels ascending and descending its
steps. When he awoke from his dream, Jacob said, "Surely the Lord is
in this place, and I knew it not." Jacob was frightened. He said, "How
full of awe is this place. This is none other than the house of God, and
this is the gate of heaven." Jacob took the stone he had used as a pil-
low and set it up as a pillar and poured oil on top of it. He named that
place Beth-El, the house of God (Genesis 28:16–19).

The ladder in Jacob's dream symbolizes the connection between the
physical world and the spiritual world, between the finitude of matter
and the infinity of spirit. These two seemingly opposite domains are
connected and related to each other. At the instant of that recognition,
Jacob understood that he was in a special place, a sacred place, where
God had revealed Himself to him. Jacob's immediate response was
to take a simple rock, upon which he had rested his head when he
slept, and sanctify it, making it a symbol of God's presence on earth.
Certainly God cannot be limited to a particular stone or any other specific place. God transcends space just as He transcends time. Yet Jacob
consecrated the place so that this physical space was also the "gate of
heaven."

The story dramatically demonstrates a key feature of religious understanding and experience. God cannot be limited to a particular space;
yet a human being can set aside a place and recognize it to be sacred,
a point of connection with the Almighty God. Human understanding
cannot comprehend the vastness of God without being overcome with
overwhelming fear and trembling. But a sacred space, being limited
and comprehensible, enables one to deal with the physical universe
and with God.

Of course, the entire universe is sacred since it is a manifestation of
God's will and power. Yet by designating a special sanctity to specific
places, the religious person creates a new spiritual reality, a new gate to
heaven. Sacred and non-sacred space may appear objectively to be the
same, but within the mind of a religious person, they are different kinds
of worlds.

Threshold

Mircea Eliade has described a threshold as "the limit, the boundary, the frontier that distinguishes and opposes two worlds and at the same time the paradoxical place where those worlds communicate, where passage from the profane to the sacred world becomes possible."[3] It is not surprising, therefore, that the threshold is a place of significance in the traditions of many peoples.

Since the home is the main base of human life, it occupies a special, private kind of space, different from the public domain outside. The Torah has commanded that the threshold of a Jewish home be graced with a mezuzah, an encased piece of parchment inscribed with the first two paragraphs of the *Sh'ma*. The mezuzah is not an amulet or a good luck charm. Its purpose is to differentiate clearly between the outside domain and the sacred, private domain of the home. By seeing the mezuzah whenever one enters or leaves the home, one is reminded of the presence of God and the commandments of the Torah. Among some Jews, the custom has arisen to place one's hand on the mezuzah upon entering and leaving home and then to kiss the fingers. This is a way of consciously absorbing the message of the mezuzah as one passes from one kind of space to another.

The Home

The Jewish home should reflect sanctity. It should contain sacred books. It should be the place where family members study Torah together, where they deepen their emotional connections to each other and to their tradition.

The table upon which the family eats is compared to an altar of God. It demands respect, blessing before and after meals, and appropriate conversation at mealtime.

It is customary among many Jews to have a special wall hanging hung on an eastern wall. This is to remind the family of the direction of Jerusalem when they pray at home.

A Jewish home is a sacred place.

The Synagogue and Study Hall

Buildings dedicated to prayer and the study of Torah are considered by Jewish tradition to be sacred places. The world inside these buildings is qualitatively different from the world outside.

The *Shulhan Arukh*, the classic code of Jewish law, has a special section on the sanctity of the synagogue (*Orah Hayyim* 151). The laws indicate the separateness and specialness of these sacred structures. It is forbidden to act in a lightheaded fashion in synagogues and study halls. Silly laughter, extraneous conversation, and eating and drinking are forbidden in these holy precincts. One is not supposed to enter them in order to get out of the sun or out of the rain, since these places are not to be used simply for one's convenience. Funerals are not to take place in synagogues except in the case of outstanding rabbis and communal leaders. One is not allowed to use the synagogue or study hall as a pathway; but if one has to pass through these buildings, one must stop to recite some sacred literature.

The sanctity of these buildings is not only exemplified by the rules of behavior in them; their actual physical structures are also accorded sanctity. For example, the *Shulhan Arukh* notes that it is customary to keep synagogues and study halls clean and to light candles in them as a sign of honor. Even after sacred buildings have been destroyed, they retain their holiness. Just as we are obligated to treat them respectfully when they are standing, so we are obligated to honor them even when they are in ruins. If grass and weeds are growing out of the ruins, we are not allowed to pull them out; rather, we must let them continue to grow in order to create within us a sense of sadness. This will inspire us to rebuild them as soon as possible, rather than to leave them in a state of ruin.

Interestingly, the study hall is considered to be more sacred than the synagogue. If a community decides to convert its synagogue into a study hall, they may do so, since they are elevating the holiness of the building. However, if they wish to convert a study hall into a synagogue, they may not do so. Torah study is a more sacred value than prayer.

The Cemetery

In Jewish tradition, the cemetery constitutes a sacred space. The land of the cemetery is considered to be consecrated; to be denied burial in a Jewish cemetery is a serious punishment for a religiously sensitive Jew.

According to the ancient laws of purity enumerated in the Torah, a priest (*cohen*) is not allowed to enter the precincts of a cemetery except in the case of the burial of a near relative. Everyone who enters a cemetery becomes ritually unclean and must undergo a ritual purification. Today the practice is to wash one's hands after leaving a cemetery. The laws of purity are a clear signal that the cemetery occupies a different kind of space from the territory outside its boundaries. It has the paradoxical status of being both consecrated and, at the same time, a source of ritual impurity.

That a cemetery is held to be sacred space is evident even from popular language usage. If tombstones are thrown over or defaced, if the land of a cemetery is treated disrespectfully, we say that the cemetery has been desecrated. Moreover, our behavior in a cemetery reflects the belief that this is a separate, special segment of space. Jewish tradition prescribes that one should not eat in a cemetery nor act in a lightheaded manner. The cemetery is the place for burial of people who have died, but also for holy books and objects that have become too worn out to be used. Thus, the cemetery is a place for reverence

Among North African Jews, there arose a custom known as *hiloula*. This is an annual pilgrimage to the grave of a saintly person. It was believed that the spirit of a righteous person continued to exert influence on the living. For example, there is an annual *hiloula* at the grave of Rabbi Amram ben Diwan in Asjen, Morocco. Rabbi Amram was an eighteenth-century Israeli sage who travelled to Morocco to raise funds for the Jewish communities in the Holy Land. While he was on his travels, his son became deathly ill. Rabbi Amram prayed that his son's life be spared, and volunteered his own life as a substitute for that of his son. And so it was: Rabbi Amram died and his son recovered. His saintliness and his ability to intercede with the Almighty made a great impression on the Jews of Morocco, and his grave became venerated.

At a *hiloula*, bonfires are lit, passages of mystical texts are read, and prayers are offered. The general mood is festive rather than somber, but the underlying message of the event is to stress the eternal value of saintliness. Death does not end one's spiritual influence on earth.

As an act of personal devotion, many people have the custom of visiting graves of parents or other close relatives, especially during the week before Rosh Hashanah. These visits have a religious quality to them and further underscore the sense of sanctity that pervades a cemetery.

Personally Sacred Places

The Talmud teaches that we are obligated to recite a blessing when we see a place where miracles were performed for our ancestors (*Berakhot* 54a). These places call to mind God's providence and are therefore to be treated with awe and devotion. The blessing praises God "who performed miracles for our ancestors in this place." Likewise, if one comes to a place where a miracle has happened to him personally, he should recite a blessing to God "who has performed for me a miracle in this place." Children and grandchildren should also say a blessing where a miracle happened to their parents and grandparents (*Shulhan Arukh, Orah Hayyim* 218).

Some sages who were saved from danger had the custom of observing the anniversary of their salvation with meditation and thanksgiving prayers to God. They celebrated this occasion with friends and relatives in order to highlight the significance of the event. Moses Maimonides had the custom of spending the day in meditation on an anniversary of a near catastrophe, and on the next day he would rejoice.[4] These anniversary observances took place even though one did not actually return to the site where the miracle occurred. The sanctity of the place was acknowledged even if one was not able to be there.

Israel, the Holy Land

Jewish tradition ascribes holiness to the land of Israel, in distinction to all other lands in the world. This is evident from the widespread custom of Jews arranging for burial in Israel or of placing some earth from Israel in the coffin of one who is buried outside Israel. There is a deep mystical belief that even in death a Jew should be associated with the special holiness of the land of Israel.

Jewish law also distinguishes between Israel and the other lands. This is especially true in the agricultural laws outlined in the Torah. The tithes, gifts to the priests, first fruits, the sabbatical year, the jubilee year—all these laws apply by Torah law only to the land of Israel. Jews involved in agriculture outside of Israel are generally exempted from these rules. Since these lands do not share in the sanctity of the land of Israel, they do not share in the specific commandments relating to the land.

Because the land of Israel is sacred, the Talmud has lengthy discussions to determine the exact boundaries of Israel. Which territories are included in the holiness and which are excluded? Since ancient Syria adjoined Israel, and since many Jews lived in that adjacent land, some of the agricultural laws of Israel were also extended to Syria. Yet living within the boundaries of Israel is considered to be a fulfillment of a biblical commandment.

Jerusalem

Jerusalem is known in Jewish liturgy as *Ir Hakodesh,* the holy city. Throughout the ages, Jews have made pilgrimages to Jerusalem and have felt that this is the city par excellence for sanctity. Jews pray facing in the direction of Jerusalem.

Within Jerusalem, the location of the ancient Temple is the holiest area. Within the Temple precincts, there were gradations of sanctity, the highest being the "Holy of Holies," a section where the high priest entered only once a year, on Yom Kippur. Popular Jewish tradition has identified the location of the Temple as being the same site where Abraham was prepared to offer his son Isaac as a sacrifice. So this place has very profound religious significance to religious Jews.

We have seen, then, that not all places share the same degree of sanctity. A religious Jew lives in a world dotted with sacred spaces.

The physical universe, for all its vastness, is not terrifying but awe-inspiring. There are landmarks that serve as bridges between the physical world and the spiritual world. These sacred places are very much like the ladder in Jacob's dream: they are rooted in the ground, but they are at the same time the gates of heaven.

5

THE RHYTHMS OF
EVERYDAY LIFE

The normal rhythms of daily activity are linked by Jewish tradition to spirituality. God, as Creator and Providential Provider, is called to mind throughout the day. The religious person lives simultaneously in the world of reality and a world of transcendence. Everything reflects deeper meanings.

A verse in Psalm 16 has been a religious guide to Jews for centuries: "I set the Lord always before me." Jewish mystics have used this verse as the theme for a special prayer design that has been incorporated in their prayer books and that has also been used as a wall hanging. Known as *Shiviti* (I have set), this design is believed to have tremendous spiritual power, elevating the worshipper to a high level of awareness of God. Its power does not necessarily stem from the combination of words or the type of design; rather, it serves to remind the individual that God is always near, always available, always watching. This consciousness of God's presence is a basic feature of Jewish religious life.

Another verse teaches a similar lesson. "In all your ways know Him" (Proverbs 3:6). Knowledge of God is an omnipresent responsibility. Heightening one's awareness of God, even in the humdrum activities of daily life, is a challenge that Jewish tradition meets in a variety of ways.

In the fifth chapter of his introduction to the *Ethics of the Fathers*, Maimonides states the Jewish attitude clearly: "A person should always place before his eyes one goal, namely the understanding of the Name, blessed be He, according to the ability of a person to know this." All of a person's activities should be directed to this single goal. Eating, drinking, sleeping, waking—all should be with the aim of strengthening one's body. The purpose of good health is to help one devote more effort to wisdom and to spiritual pursuits. And the purpose of these is to help one attain a deeper understanding of God. Maimonides notes that very few people can reach this level, where their every activity is directly linked to knowledge of God; yet this is the goal for which to strive. One who reaches it approaches the level of the prophets.

The codes of Jewish law teach that one's actions should be for the sake of Heaven. The daily rhythms of human life are intertwined with the daily rhythms of religious life.

Waking and Sleeping

Upon awaking, one should recite:

> *I thank You, ever-living divine King,*
> *that in Your love You have awakened my soul within me.*
> *Great is Your trustworthiness.*[1]

Just as we open our eyes, as we regain our consciousness after emerging from sleep, we immediately express gratitude to God for having awakened us and restored to us our soul, our consciousness. We recognize God's constant vigilance over us.

The Talmudic sages prescribed a number of blessings to be recited upon arising in the morning. Although these blessings are often recited in synagogue today at the beginning of morning services, they were originally to be recited in connection with the activities of getting up. The first blessing praises God for having given the rooster the ability to distinguish between night and day. This was to be said when one heard the crow of the rooster in the morning. Subsequent blessings praise God for the progressive stages in our awaking and getting ready for the new day: for opening our eyes, for allowing us to rise from bed, for straightening up our bodies when we stand, for clothing us, for providing solid ground upon which we can walk, for arranging our steps, for caring for all our needs, for girding us, for crowning Israel with glory (a reference to tefillin).

The above blessings are preceded by a paragraph which acknowledges that God created our soul in purity and will one day take it back and restore it to us in the world-to-come. The paragraph ends with a blessing to God "who returns souls to dead corpses." The meaning of this blessing is that we compare our sleeping body with a dead body. During sleep, it is as though we have given our soul to God for safekeeping. When we awaken, it is as though the soul is returned to our body, which until then has been "dead." This blessing underscores our absolute dependence on God for our very lives.

Upon awaking, we thank God for restoring our soul to us; upon going to sleep we pray that God will protect us during our sleep and return us to life in the morning. Before reciting the *Sh'ma*, which declares the unity of God (and which is also supposed to be recited by a dying person just before death), we say a little prayer that includes the following words:

> *May it be Your will to lay me down in peace*
> *and to raise me up again to happy and peaceful life with my portion*
> *in Your Torah....*
> *Lighten my eyes again that I sleep not the sleep of death.*

The prayers upon waking and going to sleep reflect the keen awareness of the finitude of human life in contrast to the Almighty and Eternal God. When one really confronts one's total dependence on God, one lives life in a religious spirit. One is not apt to be arrogant or self-important. Humility leads to a calmness about one's own life and a greater tolerance for the lives of others.

Ridding One's Wastes

A natural function of the human organism is to rid its wastes. This activity occurs to everyone throughout the course of the day. In our culture, it is associated with privacy and perhaps even a degree of shame. We have developed a variety of euphemisms and slang words to describe the perfectly natural function of ridding our wastes.

Our sensitivity to this part of our lives is understandable. Ridding our wastes is the ultimate reminder of our biological existence. In the words of Ernest Becker, "excreting is the curse that threatens madness because it shows man his abject finitude, his physicality, the likely unreality of his hopes and dreams."[2] It is difficult to imagine oneself as being in the image of God when in the process of excreting.

Jewish tradition has certainly been aware of this ambiguity of feeling toward ridding one's wastes. Yet it has seen in this very mundane biological function another sign of God's providence and wisdom. A blessing is to be recited:

> Blessed are You, Lord our God, King of the universe.
> In wisdom You have formed humans,
>   creating within them innumerable channels.
> In Your sublimity You know that were they rent or obstructed
>   we could not subsist even for a short while.
> Blessed are You, Lord, who works the miracle of healing for all
>   flesh.

So Jewish spiritual life also includes the rhythm of ridding our wastes.

Clothing

Jewish law and custom prescribe modest dress for men and women. Moreover, the Torah includes several laws specifically relating to clothes. It prohibits wearing clothing that has been woven from wool and flax. Known as sha'atnez, this mixture of material seems to have no intrinsic quality that warrants this prohibition. It is generally regarded as a divine law that has no reason apparent to human understanding. Yet the general prohibition can be understood as a way of making us conscious of the type of clothes we wear. Since clothing is such a basic human necessity, our concern with sha'atnez keeps our religious awareness intact even when we make, buy, or wear clothes. Another interesting law of the Torah prescribes that *tsitsit* (fringes) be attached to the corners of four-cornered garments. The laws of *tsitsit* are extensive and we will not go into them here. However, the Torah teaches that the purpose of the *tsitsit* is to serve as a reminder of all God's commandments. By looking at them, one immediately remembers the Torah's instructions—and it is one's own clothes that serve this vital function.

In biblical times, the *tsitsit* included one blue thread along with seven white ones. The Hebrew phrase *uritem oto* is generally thought to mean "and you will see it [the *tsitsit*] and thereby remember God's commandments." The Talmudic sage Rabbi Meir was puzzled by the word *oto,* a singular term. The phrase should have read *otam,* plural. He commented, therefore, that the verse is actually teaching that one who fulfills the commandment of *tsitsit* is considered to have received the Divine Presence, since the blue of the *tsitsit* resembles the sea, and the sea resembles the sky, and the sky resembles the Throne of Glory. The word *oto* refers to the single strand of blue in the *tsitsit* (*Sifrei* on Numbers 15:39). Some commentators have understood the word *oto* as deriving from the Hebrew word *ot,* meaning sign. According to this understanding, the verse is teaching that one who sees the *tsitsit* is seeing the sign of God, or God's seal. To have such a sign affixed to one's clothes is amazingly significant and impressive. Even our clothes lead us to a relationship with God.

Eating

One of the most basic rhythms of daily life is eating. Humans eat in order to maintain their bodies, but also to provide pleasure to themselves. The preparation of food so that it is pleasant to eat and to behold has played an important part in human civilization since antiquity. Food has a biological role in our lives, and also a social meaning.

Since we need food to sustain our lives, Jewish tradition has a blessing upon eating every type of food. These blessings reflect the awareness that it is God who provides us with our sustenance. They are not so much statements of thanksgiving as of awe at God's greatness. For example, the blessing for bread is:

Blessed are You, Lord our God, King of the universe,
who brings forth bread from the earth.

God gives the earth power to produce grain that can be made into bread. The blessing on fruit praises God "who creates the fruit of the trees." The blessing on vegetables lauds God "who creates the produce of the earth." The blessing over foods that do not derive from vegetation (i.e., meat, milk, water, etc.) praises God since "all came into being through His word."

Not only are blessings to be recited before eating, but a grace should be recited after eating as well. The full grace after meals is recited upon concluding a meal in which one has eaten bread. A shorter grace is pronounced after eating certain fruits or baked goods (other than bread), and after drinking wine. After eating other things, the following blessing is to be recited:

Blessed are You, Lord our God, King of the universe,
Creator of souls innumerable and their needs,
for all that You have created to keep every living soul in life;
blessed is the everlasting God.

These blessings praise God for maintaining our biological existence. Virtually every time we eat, we alert ourselves to God the Creator of the universe, God the sustainer of our lives. Religious sensitivity and awe are linked to the human rhythm of eating.

But Jewish tradition goes beyond this. The Torah lists which animals are permissible to be eaten and which are forbidden. The laws of kashrut clearly delineate two categories of foods: the permitted and the forbidden. Among the forbidden are animals that do not chew their cud nor have split hooves; fish without fins and scales; foods prepared of a mixture of meat and dairy. Moreover, even permitted animals may not be eaten unless properly slaughtered according to Jewish law. The laws of kashrut are quite extensive and play a significant role in the lives of religious Jews. We may not put any food into our mouths without first knowing that it is kosher. This is an impressive reality. It involves a constant consciousness of the ingredients of the food we buy, of the food served to us; it entails knowledge of the sources of any meat or fish we eat; it involves keeping our kitchens in such a way that meat and milk items are kept separate. There is no other such comprehensive regimen in the daily life of the religious Jew.

In terms of the pleasure of food, Jewish tradition has recognized the role of food in generating happiness and good feelings. A Talmudic statement teaches that "there is no happiness except with meat and wine." Shabbat and festivals are to be celebrated with festive meals. The Talmudic sage Shammai was said to have set the proper example by buying the best food he could find in the market for his Shabbat meals. If he bought the best food one day and on the next day found something better, he would buy the better merchandise for Shabbat and eat his first purchase on a weekday. The very celebration of eating is considered a fulfillment of God's commandment to enjoy the holy days.

The symbols surrounding eating reflect the sanctity associated with this basic human experience. The table upon which one eats is considered symbolically to be as the altar in the Temple in Jerusalem. It is consecrated. One is not supposed to treat a table with disrespect, to sit on it, to place one's shoes on it. Before eating a meal, we ritually wash our hands as a sign of purification. Just as Jews entering the Temple in ancient Jerusalem had to purify themselves before coming to the altar, so we must do likewise. We recite the blessing over bread, but before eating it we dip it in salt. This is reminiscent of the practice in the Temple to add salt to the sacrifices offered on the altar.

Sephardim introduce the Grace after Meals (when at least three have eaten together) with a verse stating that "this is the table that is before the Lord." This is a further reminder of the sanctity of the table and of the reverence we are supposed to have when eating.

The Menstrual Cycle

Women experience a monthly biological rhythm. From the age of puberty until menopause, women are physically and emotionally involved in this rhythm. The menstrual cycle is governed by an inner clock; women experience this connection with the passage of time and the rhythm of physical life in a more direct way than men.

The Torah has traditionally taught that a woman is considered ritually impure during her menstrual period. Sexual relations with her husband are forbidden during this time of the month. The practice adopted since Talmudic times has been for women to wait seven clean days following their period. Then they go to a *mikvah* (a ritual bath) to immerse themselves. Only after the ritual ablution may they resume normal marital relations with their husbands. At the time of the immersion, a blessing is recited acknowledging that God has commanded this form of purification.

Since the menstrual cycle is such a basic feature of a woman's life, and since it recurs regularly at fairly short intervals, it is only to be expected that Jewish religiosity is connected to it. It is part of the mystery of the life process, part of the rhythm of life. A woman during her period becomes separated in certain ways from her normal pattern of life. Her awareness of her bodily functions intensifies. Her recognition of God as Creator should be heightened. Once she has finished her period and waited the seven days following, she immerses in the *mikvah*. Symbolically, she emerges from the natural water as a newborn child, with a sense of awe and amazement. The *mikvah* experience is a renewal for those who observe it properly. It significantly deepens one's connection with a natural life rhythm and with the God who created this rhythm.

The Miracle of the Daily Rhythms of Life

The *Amidah*, the silent prayer that is recited three times daily, includes a paragraph of thanksgiving to God. It praises God

> *for our lives entrusted to Your hand,*
> *for our souls in Your care,*

for Your wonders ever with us,
and for Your marvelous goodness toward us at all times,
morning, noon and night.

Religious rituals deepen our awareness of the providence of God and of our continuous relationship with Him.

The rhythms of daily life are not taken for granted. From our waking and sleeping to ridding our wastes, to dressing and to eating—all are windows to a greater awareness of God. Jewish spirituality is intimately connected with these daily rhythms and cannot be divorced from them. We strive always to place God before us, to know Him in all our ways.

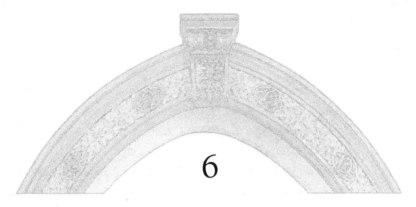

6

HALAKHAH, THE JEWISH WAY OF LIFE

Jewish religious tradition provides symbols and observances to bring one into as full an awareness of God's presence as possible. The natural world unfolds the glory of God the Creator, but one can grow accustomed to the phenomena of nature and take them for granted much of the time. Halakhah, Jewish law, adds a dimension of specificity to Jewish spirituality. It is not merely a poetic, artistic experience; it also involves specific activities to do and not to do. The halakhah, which literally means "the path to walk," is a full system and guide for life; through its precepts, the Jew is in a continuous relationship with God.

Halakhah can be understood as the way God wants the people of Israel to conduct their lives. The specific laws, customs, and traditions of the Jews must be seen in the context of this definition. If one studies or observes the details of halakhah without full awareness of its divine source, one misses its real meaning.

How do we know God's will, what He wants the people of Israel to do? We know from God's own revealed words, the Torah. The written Torah was accompanied by an oral law, *Torah she'be'al peh*. The original oral law provided explanations and clarifications of the Torah; it also provided the basis for future interpretation of the Torah by the rabbinic authorities of the Great Court.[1]

One category of the oral Torah includes explanations of the Torah that were given by God to Moses. For example, in Leviticus 23:40 the

Torah commands in regard to Sukkot: "And you shall take on the first day the fruit of a beautiful tree, branches of palm trees, and boughs of thick trees and willows of the brook, and you shall rejoice before the Lord your God seven days." The verse does not specify which fruit from a beautiful tree should be taken. Nor does it give the specifications for the other items to be taken: how many palm branches, how many boughs, in what condition, for how long? Yet Moses must have received instruction from God concerning these details, since it was his job to teach the law to the people of Israel. Therefore, we must conclude that God conveyed to Moses the necessary information. For example, the "fruit of the beautiful tree" is an etrog (citron); when we take an etrog on Sukkot we are fulfilling the will of God as expressed in this commandment both through the written and oral Torah.

Another example is from Deuteronomy 6:8, where we learn that the words of the Torah are to be bound "as a sign upon your hand and as frontlets between your eyes." But how is this verse to be understood? Since the language is vague and open to interpretation, Moses must have received clarification from God originally. The oral law explains this verse to be referring to tefillin and provides the details: tefillin must be made of leather, must be black, and must include certain biblical passages.

The oral interpretations of the Torah are intrinsic to the understanding of the written Torah. Indeed, they are also expressions of God's will. Halakhah in its pure sense, then, goes directly back to the word of God as expressed in the Torah and in the oral explanations of the Torah given to Moses.

The words of the Torah, even with their ancient explanations, still leave many questions unanswered. The language of the Torah is not legalistic for the most part. Even in its legalistic sections, it is not precise as a code of law. The words of the Torah demand explanation and interpretation. The Torah provides us with the word of God, but also leaves much room for human interpretation and application of principles. Due to changed conditions and/or perceptions, the words of the Torah are not always easily applied to contemporary life. Therefore, the halakhah also includes categories of rabbinic law. The rabbis of each generation are given the responsibility and authority to apply the teachings of the Torah to their own situation. Categories of rabbinic law include:

- Laws derived by hermeneutic principles, by interpretations of the Torah
- Rabbinical ordinances
- Local regulations and customs

These categories of halakhah are not based directly on God's command, but on the rabbinic application of Torah principles to their contemporary situations. The Torah and the original oral law represent God's words to Israel; the rabbinic categories of halakhah represent the effort of human beings to derive God's will from the principles of the Torah.

The Great Court in Jerusalem

Since Jewish life is entirely involved in halakhah, it is necessary for Jews to know exactly what the halakhah requires of them. The role of rabbis and teachers has always been to elucidate the halakhah, to deal with practical and theoretical halakhic questions brought to them by interested Jews.

In ancient Israel, there was a Great Court in Jerusalem, popularly known as the Sanhedrin, which was the recognized authoritative body to pronounce the halakhah. Whenever a controversy arose involving Jewish law in Israel, local rabbinic courts would pass judgment to resolve it. When the controversy was too difficult to handle on the local level, it was brought before the Great Court in Jerusalem and was solved there. There was no further recourse. The decision of the Great Court was authoritative.

The Great Court not only responded to problems brought to it, but also devoted itself to studying the Torah and establishing how the Torah laws should be applied. The Great Court performed judicial and legislative functions.

Moses Maimonides, in his classic code of halakhah, describes the Great Court in the following terms:

> The Great Court in Jerusalem represents the essence of the oral Torah. Its members are the pillars of direction; law and order emanate from them to all of Israel. And upon them the Torah rests its trust, as it says: "You shall act in accordance with the directions they give you" (Deuteronomy 17:11). This is a positive commandment; anyone who believes in Moses our teacher and in his Torah is obligated to rely upon them in matters of religion and to depend on them. (*Laws of Rebels* 1:1)

The Great Court in Jerusalem, then, was the institution which preserved and developed all aspects of the oral law. It maintained the ancient traditions going back to Moses, and also added its own interpretations, ordinances, and customs in order to guide the lives of the Israelites.

The Great Court had the authority to interpret the Torah and to declare its judgment concerning the will of God. Yet interpretations could change from one generation to the next; the oral law would retain fluidity and flexibility. Maimonides writes:

> A Great Court which interpreted scripture using one of the principles of interpretation, and ruled according to the way it seemed to them that the law should be—their judgment is the law. If a subsequent Great Court found a reason to refute their decision, it should refute it and judge according to the way it seems to them, as it says "to the judge who will be in those days"—you are only obligated to follow the Court which is in your generation. (*Laws of Rebels* 2:1)

Under certain circumstances, the Great Court even had the power to overrule a law of the Torah (see, for example, the discussion in the Talmud, *Yevamot* 90b). Each Court had the right and responsibility to use its own understanding in applying the word of God to the life of the people of Israel. When the Great Court of Jerusalem ceased to operate and the Jews were exiled by the Romans (70 CE), a group of rabbis attempted to reestablish authority in a rabbinical court in Yavneh. The effort was important but short-lived. After the Bar Kokhba rebellion (135 CE) many of the leading sages were executed by the Romans; and the establishment of a central authoritative rabbinic court proved unfeasible. Rabbi Yehudah the Prince, in the mid-second century CE, compiled the Mishnah, a record of the oral law up to his time. From then on, the Mishnah became the central text in halakhah; rabbis no longer derived laws directly from the text of the Torah, but focused their studies and decisions on the text of the Mishnah. Rabbinical discussions of the Mishnah became known as the Gemara; the Mishnah and Gemara together are known as the Talmud. The Talmud became the basis of all halakhic discussions and decisions.

Over the generations, many other layers of rabbinic scholarship have been added to halakhic literature. In general terms, these include the writings of the Geonim (scholars of Babylonia, sixth through tenth centuries); Rishonim (eleventh through fifteenth centuries); and Aharonim (sixteenth through nineteenth centuries); as well as modern contemporary sages.

The dissolution of the Great Court changed the method of halakhah. No longer was there one universally recognized institution that could rule authoritatively for all Jews. No longer did rabbis go directly to the Torah in order to determine halakhah. Instead of having an oral law that could be somewhat fluid, halakhah became based on written texts and was increasingly dependent on precedents. For example, no rabbi of any reputation today will write a responsum without quoting earlier authorities and the Talmud before presenting his own decision. Seldom will the Torah itself be cited to prove a point of law.

A Modern Sanhedrin?

As has been seen, the process of the halakhah underwent a significant change with the loss of the Great Court. Rabbis and laymen have not had a central religious body to resolve their dilemmas. Amazingly,

Jews have flourished for nearly two thousand years in many different lands without having a central institution of halakhah. In spite of differences of custom and emphasis that have arisen among different groups of Jews, the essential unity of halakhah was preserved. To this day, every Jew who adheres to halakhah shares in a truly remarkable historic, religious, sociological, spiritual, and national enterprise.

There have been some individuals who have called for the establishment of a new Sanhedrin in our times. They would like a revival of a universal halakhic authority for the Jewish people. The Sanhedrin would not only provide unity in halakhah, but would reinstitute the original methodology of the oral law—interpreting the Torah itself, applying the law to life with the freedom to overrule precedents and previous decisions.

One of those calling for a Sanhedrin was the Sephardic Chief Rabbi of Israel, Rabbi Benzion Uziel (1880–1953). In a speech delivered on 12 Kislev 5697 (November 26, 1936), he called for an authoritative rabbinic body along the lines of the Great Court of Jerusalem.[2] He viewed this effort as a continuation of the work of Rabbi Yohanan ben Zakkai, who had been instrumental in establishing a quasi-Sanhedrin in Yavneh following the destruction of Jerusalem by the Romans.

Rabbi Uziel believed it was the responsibility of the rabbinate to work to achieve this goal. Rabbis are delegated the responsibility of establishing *mishpat* (justice). This refers not only to cases between contending individuals, but also to public issues, questions of taxation, and communal needs. By working for a Sanhedrin, the rabbis would be working for a unifying force in Jewish life. Rabbi Uziel argued that one who simply knew how to rule on what is permitted and what is forbidden, or on who is guilty and who is innocent—such a person is not truly in the category of being a *posek*, a decider of halakhah. This person is known as a *talmid* or *talmid haham,* a student or a wise student. To be a *posek*, however, involves having the power of the Great Court. Only the Sanhedrin can serve as a real *posek*. "The responsibility of the Sanhedrin was to clarify and distinguish between true interpretations (which are true to the spirit of the Torah) and casuistic interpretations (which are erroneous)."[3]

Rabbi Uziel writes that the *posek* draws conclusions from the Torah and the words of the prophets, as well as from the traditional oral law.

> The *posek* in Israel is not bound by precedents of the *posek* of laws who precedes him. If he was, this would lead to great damage, in that an accidental error would be fixed as a permanent halakhah even though it was erroneous in its foundation. In order to avoid this harmful eventuality, the authority of the Great Court was restricted only to the time in which it sits on the chair of judgment. But the decisions of the Great Court are not established as law and do not obligate the judges who will come after them to judge and to teach like them.[4]

Rabbi Uziel was deeply impressed by the work of Moses Maimonides and believed that he deserved the title *posek*. Maimonides worked to make the laws of the Torah known to the general public. In his comprehensive code of Jewish law, Maimonides recorded the halakhah anonymously to signify that it represents a consensus, not just the opinion of individuals. He not only gathered his material from all rabbinic literature, but he also derived benefit from the teachings of non-Jewish thinkers.

> In this matter, by the way, Maimonides has informed us that in halakhic decisions one must comprehend all things on the basis of their content and truth, and not on the authority of their authors alone. Maimonides taught a great principle: Accept the truth from those who have stated it.[5]

In order to restore a central authority for halakhah, Rabbi Uziel urged:

> Let us arise and establish the Great Court in Jerusalem, not in order to judge cases of fines, or capital cases, and not in order to permit the first-born because of its blemish. Rather, let us do so in order to solve the questions of life which confront us each day in our settlements and in our world; and in order to create a

beginning for our destined redemption: "And I will return your judges as in the beginning and your advisers as formerly; for out of Zion will the Torah proceed and the word of God from Jerusalem."[6]

Until a Great Court is reestablished in Jerusalem, the halakhah is taught by leading rabbinical sages who draw on the vast rabbinic literature that has developed over the past several thousand years. There are variations of opinion on details of halakhah—different sages rule differently—yet the halakhic process continues to provide the framework for religious Jewish life. In order for a sage to be recognized as authoritative, he must not only have great erudition; he must not only be personally observant of halakhah; but he must also be fully faithful to the idea that halakhah is the expression of the will of God to the Jewish people. Halakhah, therefore, must be taken seriously on its own terms.

A Sephardic Approach to Halakhah

Without a Great Court in Jerusalem, it was only natural that different approaches to halakhah developed among various Jewish communities during the past nearly two thousand years.[7] Customs and practices varied from place to place and from time to time. Attitudes toward halakhic study also differed. Certainly the basic assumptions of the divine origin of the Torah and the authority of halakhah were accepted; but differences in style definitely did exist among religious Jewish communities throughout the ages.

Two major streams of Jewish tradition are the Ashkenazic and the Sephardic. Ashkenazim primarily lived in Europe (*Ashkenaz* means Germany in Hebrew). In the Middle Ages they were concentrated in France, Germany, and Italy. Gradually, the centers of Ashkenazic Jewry shifted to Poland, Russia, and Eastern Europe in general. The common feature of these communities is that they existed in Christian countries.

The Westernization of these communities was intensified during the eighteenth and nineteenth centuries, when European Jews were gain-ing rights of citizenship in the countries in which they lived. The doors of Western civilization opened to them as never before; Jews studied in European universities; they advanced in professional, cultural, and political life. However, their struggles for civil rights were painful and not fully successful. Anti-Jewish attitudes and actual violence against Jews ultimately led many Ashkenazim to migrate to Israel, the United States, and other safe havens. The Nazi Holocaust during World War II decimated European Jewry, most of which was of Ashkenazic background. Yet Ashkenazic Jewry today represents a large majority of world Jewry.

Ashkenazic numerical dominance has been matched by its cultural hegemony as well. Certainly for the past three centuries and more, Ashkenazic rabbis have dominated halakhah; Ashkenazic thinkers have dominated Jewish philosophy; Ashkenazic writers and artists have dominated Jewish cultural life.

The Sephardic Jews enjoyed their period of dominance during the centuries prior to the expulsion of Jews from Spain in 1492 (*Sepharad* refers to Spain in Hebrew). The contributions of Sephardim to all areas of Jewish scholarship and thought—as well as to science, medicine, and mathematics—were impressive, unequalled in the Jewish world. Even during the century following the expulsion, Sephardic Jewry maintained a dynamic spiritual and cultural life that influenced world Jewry.

The considerable majority of Sephardim who left the Iberian Peninsula settled in Muslim countries. Although Sephardim also went to Italy, Holland, France, and other Western European locations, the much greater number flourished in non-Western environments. The Ottoman Empire provided a haven for Sephardic refugees. Sephardic communities developed throughout Turkey, the Balkan countries, the Middle East, and North Africa. Their experience was different in many ways from that of the Ashkenazim of Europe. Indeed, the two groups of Jews lived in relative isolation from each other.

Although it is difficult to generalize about differences in the realm of halakhah, it may be argued that there were different trends of halakhic thinking among the two groups, just as there were differences in worldviews in general. It is of interest to explore the Sephardic approach to halakhah, since it may serve as an alternative to the prevailing Ashkenazic approach. Since Sephardim lived among non-Western people, their perceptions and attitudes about Judaism may serve as a counterbalance to the preponderant Westernization of Judaism.

A people's attitudes are often conveyed through their words and actions when they are not self-conscious about being observed. They are implied in proverbs and songs, in the way people dress, in their gestures, in the way they express themselves. In order to comprehend a Sephardic approach to halakhah, one must attempt to grasp the undocumented, non-explicit elements of Sephardic culture, elements that are known from sharing a people's mentality.

One element that needs to be considered is joie de vivre. While Sephardim living in Muslim lands over the past four centuries were generally quite observant of halakhah, their observance did not lead them to become somber or overly serious. Pious Sephardim sang Judeo-Spanish love ballads and drinking songs at family celebrations in a natural way, without self-consciousness. Singing in a lighthearted spirit, even at public gatherings, did not strike them as being irreverent. Rather, the pleasures and aesthetics of this world were viewed in a positive light.

Sephardic holiday celebrations and lifecycle observances, for example, were characterized by the preparation of elaborate delicacies to eat, the singing of songs, and a general spirit of gaiety and hospitality. Sephardim appreciated colorful fabrics, fine embroidery, and excellent craftsmanship in metals. On every happy occasion there was bound to be the fragrance of rose water, herbs, and fresh fruits. All of these accoutrements—song, food, fragrances, decorative materials—gave the specific religious observance its distinctive quality. These things were not peripheral to halakhah, but gave halakhah its proper context: a context of love, happiness, and optimism.

This spirit carried itself even to the serious season of the High Holy Days, when self-scrutiny and repentance were expected. The travel account of Rabbi Simhah ben Joshua of Zalozhtsy (1711–1768) sheds interesting light on this fact.[8] He travelled to the Holy Land with a group of ascetic Hasidim in 1764, and the majority of his Jewish co-passengers on the ship were Sephardim. The rabbi noted that "the Sephardim awoke before daybreak to say penitential prayers in a congregation, as is their custom in the month of Elul." He then added: "During the day they eat and rejoice and are happy at heart." For Rabbi Simhah, this behavior seemed paradoxical; but the Sephardim themselves did not even realize that their behavior was in any way noteworthy. Their unstated assumption was that eating, rejoicing, and being happy of heart were not in conflict with piety, even in the serious season of penitential prayers.

Alan Watts has pointed out that in Western thought the individual is "split." One is both herself and an observer of herself. We analyze ourselves and tend to see ourselves as though we are somehow outside of ourselves. Carried to an extreme, this can be confusing and frustrating. It is as though we live our lives while seeing ourselves in a mirror. We are apt to become overly self-conscious, self-critical, and self-centered. Eastern culture, on the other hand, tends to be more holistic, less self-analytical. People are taught to live naturally and easily, without objectifying themselves overly much. Watts has written:

> The most spiritual people are the most human. They are natural
> and easy in manner; they give themselves no airs; they interest
> themselves in ordinary everyday matters, and are not forever talk-
> ing and thinking about religion. For them there is no difference
> between spirituality and usual life, and to their awakened insight
> the lives of the most humdrum and earth-bound people are as
> much in harmony with the infinite as their own.[9]

The Sephardim tended to have the Eastern, rather than the Western, attitude on life. The halakhah was observed naturally and easily, as a vital part of life. André Chouraqui, in his study of North African Jewry, has noted that the Jews of the Maghreb were quite observant of halakhah; and "the Judaism of the most conservative of the Maghreb's Jews was marked by a flexibility, a hospitality, a tolerance." The Jews of North Africa had a "touching generosity of spirit and a profound respect for meditation."[10] These comments are equally applicable to Sephardim throughout the Mediterranean area.

To borrow from the terminology of geometry, the Ashkenazim tended to prefer sharp angles, while Sephardim tended to prefer circles and rounded edges. This analogy was placed in halakhic terms by Rabbi Hayyim Yosef David Azulai (1724–1806), one of the leading rabbinic figures of his time. He wrote that in matters of halakhah, Sephardic sages clung to the quality of *hesed* (kindness), and tended to be lenient. Ashkenazim manifested the quality of *gevurah* (heroism), and therefore tended to be strict. Rabbi Azulai's statement, though a grand generalization, is a profound indication of his own self-image. He and numerous other Sephardic rabbis saw themselves as agents of *hesed*. This self-image could not but influence the manner in which they dealt with questions of halakhah. *Hesed* was not merely a pleasant idea but a working principle.

H. J. Zimmels, in his book *Ashkenazim and Sephardim*, indicates that as a general rule Sephardim were more lenient than the Ashkenazim in their halakhic rulings.[11] He suggests that the Ashkenazic inclination to stringency was largely the result of centuries of persecution suffered by German Jewry. It also stemmed from the doctrines of the German Hasidim of the twelfth and thirteenth centuries, who emphasized strictness in religious observance. Groups of Ashkenazic Jews imposed upon themselves greater stringencies than the law demanded and, in time, many of these observances became normative.

Rabbi Benzion Uziel offered an insight into the differences between Sephardic and Ashkenazic sages. Sephardic rabbis felt powerful enough in their opinion and authority to annul customs that were not based on halakhic foundations. In contrast, Ashkenazic rabbis tended to strengthen customs and sought support for them even if they seemed strange or without halakhic basis. The rabbis of France and Germany had a negative opinion of the rabbis of Spain, feeling that the Sephardic sages were too independent and too irreverent to tradition. On the other hand, the Sephardim felt that their method was correct and were quite proud of promoting it.[12]

Sephardic tradition stressed the idea that the halakhah is a practical guide to behavior. It is not a metaphysical system set aside for an intellectual elite. On the contrary, each person was entitled and obligated to understand what the halakhah requires. It is not surprising therefore that the classic codes of Jewish law were produced in Sephardic communities. Sephardic scholars studied texts with the goal of applying their rules directly to actual situations; therefore, they had to remain sensitive to the needs of people.

This very sensitivity helped maintain the quality of *hesed* in halakhah. When halakhah is studied as an intellectual system divorced from actual life situations, it may follow the dictates of logic and intricate reasoning rather than the dictates of human kindness. A legal conclusion might be reached in the abstract and then be applied to human conditions as a derrick operation from above. This approach is contrary to the overall spirit of Sephardic halakhic thought.

Although it is incumbent upon each Jew to study Torah and halakhah, difficult questions and disputes cannot always be solved by the individuals involved. Thus, over the past centuries, Sephardic communities normally appointed a chief rabbi, often referred to as *haham*, sage. He had the final word in matters of halakhah for his community. The institution of *haham* provided the Jews with a recognized authority who could resolve their questions. When the Sephardim of the Island of Rhodes wanted to appoint a chief rabbi in the early seventeenth century, they agreed that no one had the right to contest the *haham*'s rulings:

> All which he will decide will be correct and acceptable as the law which was determined by the Court of Rabban Gamliel.... All which he will decide ... will be correct and acceptable as a law of God's Torah as it was given at Sinai."[13]

The Jews of Rhodes linked their *haham*'s authority to that of the powerful court of Rabban Gamliel and to the Torah itself. Other Sephardic communities did likewise. This was a way of restoring, at least on a communal level, the original function of the Great Court in Jerusalem, which, according to Maimonides, was the essential institution of the halakhah. Rabbi Yosef Taitatsak (sixteenth century, Salonika) expressed this idea clearly: "Know that each and every community has authority over its members, for every community may legislate in its city just as the Great Court could legislate for all Israel."[14]

Law and Life

Since halakhah is an all-encompassing guide to life that describes what God wants us to do, it is essential that we understand its role in our lives. Observing the mitzvot is a Jew's way of connecting with the eternal reality of God. To treat halakhah as a mechanical system of laws is to miss its meaning and significance. Halakhah provides the framework for spiritual awareness, religious insight, and even spontaneity.

At the root of halakhah is the awareness that God is overwhelmingly great and that human beings are overwhelmingly limited. Humility is the hallmark of the truly religious person. One must be open to the spirit of God that flows through the halakhah.

A true sage must be humble; arrogance is a sign of not understanding the real lesson of halakhah. Solomon Schechter, in his beautiful essay about the mystics of Safed of the sixteenth century, quotes Shlomel of Moravia, who described the scholars, saints, and men of good deeds of Safed, indicating that many of them were worthy of receiving the Divine Spirit: "None among them is ashamed to go to the well and draw water and carry home the pitcher on his shoulders, or go to the market to buy bread, oil, and vegetables. All the work in the house is done by themselves."[15] These sages followed the model of Talmudic rabbis, who also did not find it beneath their dignity to work at menial tasks. Egotism and a sense of inflated self-importance are contrary to the spirit of Jewish religiosity.

It is interesting to note how this ideal has been somewhat diminished among Western Jews. Isidore Epstein, in his study of the responsa of Rabbi Simon Duran, displays a Western bias when he writes that

the multifarious functions of the rabbis [of North Africa] also testify to the low standards of Jewish culture of North African

Jewry. In adverting to Jewish past and present day history, we cannot fail to notice that wherever there is a strong, virile, and advanced Jewish life, there is the tendency to keep the rabbinical office distinct from other callings; and the combination of rabbinical charges with other functions is a sign of decadence and of lack of appreciation of learning as such. North Africa in our period exhibited that characteristic system of cultural decline. There the rabbi was not "rabbi" in the understood sense of the word, but combined with that office the functions of school teacher, slaughterer, and reader to the consequent lowering in his prestige and rabbinical authority."[16]

Epstein's assumption that it is a sign of decadence when rabbis assume responsibilities other than the purely academic is quite absurd. The contrary seems much truer. The Talmudic sages assumed other responsibilities as did the outstanding sages of the Sephardic world; and they did not feel demeaned thereby. It is precisely when rabbis relegate to themselves purely academic functions and when they consider it undignified to meet other communal needs that egotism and pettiness arise. It is actually to the credit of North African Jews, and many other Sephardic communities as well, that rabbis often served in practical capacities, participating more fully in the life of their communities. This was not at all a shame for them or a reflection of cultural decadence for the communities.

Humility is a virtue that halakhah fosters for sages and laypeople alike. Rabbi David ibn Abi Zimra (sixteenth century) offered an explanation of a rabbinic dictum that one is not supposed to argue with the greatest of the judges who has made a ruling on a legal question. Yet what if he is wrong? Shouldn't the lesser judges have the right and responsibility to dissent? Rabbi David ibn Abi Zimra explains that the dictum was not intended as a warning for the lesser judges but rather for the greatest judge. The judge occupying the highest position should not give his decision first because others will be afraid to argue with him. His decision will intimidate the others. Therefore, true justice demands that the greater judges withhold their opinions until the lesser ones have had their say. In this way, all opinions can be evaluated fairly, without intimidation or arrogance.[17]

In a similar spirit, Rabbi Hayyim Yosef David Azulai comments on a passage in the *Ethics of the Fathers* that teaches that each person should actively prepare to study Torah since it does not come automatically as an inheritance. Rabbi Azulai notes that each sage received a specific portion from Sinai and therefore even a great sage needs to learn from others. No scholar is self-sufficient; no sage inherits all wisdom. It is necessary for everyone to be humble, to be open to the opinions of others, to try to learn from everyone.[18]

Piety

Many wonderful and horrible things have been done in the name of religion. George Bernard Shaw once wrote: "Beware of a man whose God is in Heaven." It is difficult, perhaps impossible, to have reasonable communication with someone who feels that he knows Truth, that only those who share his beliefs are absolutely right.

There have been great prophets, mystics, and pietists who have lived their lives in relationship with God. There have also been inquisitors, murderers, and arrogant criminals who have thought that they acted according to the will of God. If religion attracts the most sensitive and thoughtful people, it also draws those who wish to seem important and holy in the eyes of others, who use the cloak of religion to hide their own egocentric purposes.

Since the Jewish religious tradition is deeply tied to halakhah, it is not surprising that there have been people who have found their self-importance in legalism. There is a fine line between pious devotion and misguided asceticism. Rabbi Azulai has taught that one should not follow unnecessary stringencies in law. Even in private, one should not be overly stringent, unless motivated by pure and humble piety.[19] Those who do accept additional obligations upon themselves should not consider themselves superior to others who do not accept such stringencies. A truly pious person feels no need to compare her personal piety to that of others; her life is lived in relationship to God; she lives with humility and equanimity.

Jewish history has witnessed the honest spirituality of innumerable pious men and women who have sincerely served God through their observance of halakhah. It has also witnessed pietistic movements, where groups of people observed Jewish law with intensity and introduced pious customs into Jewish religious life. Such movements include the German Hasidim of the thirteenth century; the Sephardic mystical schools of the sixteenth century; the Eastern-European Hasidic movement of the seventeenth century; and the Musar movement of the nineteenth century. These and other religious movements called on Jews to deepen their religious experience by intensifying their observance of halakhah and by adopting additional pious practices.

Rabbi Moshe Cordovero of sixteenth-century Safed, for example, composed a list of rules for Jews to observe. The following are some of his recommendations.[20]

- One should not turn attention from meditating on Torah and holiness, so that one's heart will constantly be a sanctuary for the Divine Presence.
- One should strive never to become angry. One should always be concerned about the needs of fellow beings and should behave kindly to them. One should behave nicely even with those who transgress the laws of the Torah.
- One should not drink wine except on Shabbat and holy days.
- One should pray with concentration.
- One should not speak badly about any person or any other living creation of God. One should never speak falsehood or even imply falsehood.
- One should meet with a friend each Friday evening to review what has occurred during the course of the past week.
- One should recite the afternoon prayer with a prayer shawl and tefillin. One should chant the Grace after Meals aloud. Each night, one should sit on the ground and lament the destruction

of the Temple in Jerusalem; and should also cry over personal sins which lengthen the time before our ultimate redemption.

- One should avoid being part of four groups which do not receive the Divine Presence: hypocrites, liars, idlers, and those who speak evil about others.
- One should give charity each day in order to atone for sins.
- One should pay pledges immediately and not postpone them.
- One should confess sins prior to eating and prior to going to sleep.
- One should fast as often as his health allows.

These rules, and other similar ones, stem from the overwhelming desire of religiously sensitive people to serve God in fullness. The more they can do, the closer they feel to the Almighty. When their deeds are observed in the spirit of love and selflessness, they are spiritually meaningful. The problem, of course, is that these rules of piety may themselves become merely mechanical observances.

The genius of halakhah is that it provides a medium for approaching God on a constant basis. Each law, each observance, is a link between the human and the Divine. But the power of halakhah cannot be appreciated without spiritual sensitivity, openness, and—above all—humility.

Saintliness

It is a rare experience to be in the presence of a truly saintly person, one who lives her life in a deep relationship with God. We might describe such a person as having wisdom, humility, inner peace, and tranquility. The saintly person lives life on a different plane from most other people.

One cannot attain saintliness as the result of following any specific prescriptions. There are no schools to educate and graduate saints. There are no rituals or techniques that, if followed, will result automatically in the creation of a genuinely pious person.

In describing the actions and observances of deeply pious people, we only describe the evident and superficial aspects of their lives. Their inner lives remain a secret to us. We are intrigued by such people because we do not fully understand their inner beings.

Following the external dictates of halakhah does not guarantee the quality of saintliness. Without mystical insight, without an all-encompassing love, the practitioner of halakhah merely mimics saintliness. Halakhah must be experienced as a fulfillment of the will of God if it is to generate spirituality.

Modern society does not place a particularly high premium on saintliness. Our society is achievement oriented, pragmatic, materially centered. Even religion is profoundly influenced by these values. Religious institutions are concerned with perpetuating themselves—raising money, obtaining members, providing services. Prayer services might pass for good (or not-so-good) theater. They may provide parodies of prayer, where people appear to be praying while having no sense of the presence of God.

It is difficult to preach about God and mystical saintliness except to unusual individuals. The ideal of halakhah is to create righteous people. Even those who may never attain the highest spiritual level still need to know what the goal is. In describing the religious life of North African Jewry, André Chouraqui has noted that the Jews of the Maghreb valued saintliness as the ultimate quality.[21] They expected their rabbis to be well-versed in Torah and rabbinic literature; but more than this, they expected them to be able to pray with sincerity and real devotion. By being in the presence of saintly teachers, average people could be raised in their own spiritual life. In a society that values saintliness as the ultimate human goal, it is more natural to achieve piety. It is far more difficult to attain saintliness in a pragmatic, materialistic culture.

Halakhah is the ever-present link between God and the Jewish people. Through observance of halakhah in the spirit of humility, the Jew has the opportunity to live on a deep, spiritual level. The goal of halakhah is to create righteous, saintly people.

7

REVELATION

God reveals Himself as Creator through the world that He has created and that He maintains. A thoughtful human being may see in natural phenomena a reflection of God. Jewish tradition ties the Jew to the rhythms of nature in order to deepen one's experience of God the Creator.

God has also revealed Himself to the people of Israel at Mount Sinai. The Torah and halakhah are reflections of the will of God. By studying the Torah and observing the halakhah, the religious Jew has a unique path to God. As has been noted in the previous chapter, the observance of halakhah is meaningful insofar as it is understood to be a fulfillment of God's will. Since halakhah is an all-embracing system of life that governs virtually every instant of life, the pious Jew has the opportunity of reaching great spiritual heights and maintaining an almost constant relationship with God.

God's revelation through nature may be experienced by all people, Jews and non-Jews alike. But nature leads us to an awe and love for the Creator while not giving us any insight as to how to conduct our lives according to His will. Revelation through the Torah comes to fill this void, to give specific direction to the Jewish people as to how they should live within a special relationship to God.

Maimonides, in his *Guide of the Perplexed*, has explained:

> Such religious acts as studying the Torah, praying, and performance of other precepts, serve exclusively as the means of causing

us to occupy and fill our mind with the precepts of God, and free it from worldly business; for we are thus, as it were, in communication with God, and undisturbed by any other thing. (*Guide of the Perplexed* III:51)

So both nature and the Torah provide paths to God. The communication that God sends to humans, though, is dependent on a person's sensitivity to hearing the message. It is possible for different people to experience the same phenomenon and have entirely different reactions. In other words, it is not just a matter of observing an objective reality, but also of experiencing it subjectively.

Yet the history of religion also records many examples of individuals who have communed with God not merely by being sensitive to nature and sacred texts, but who have claimed actually to have heard God's voice. In these communications, the originator is God and He communicates with words. Such communications are in the category of direct revelations of God. They are claimed to be objectively true, not simply subjectively meaningful experiences.

How are we to understand such revelations? It is difficult to explain in logical, reasonable terms that the eternal and infinite God speaks with words to mortal humans. Revelation cannot be proven or demonstrated by philosophy or theology, but only by first-hand experience. Yehudah Halevy argued in his *Kuzari* that the genuineness of God's revelation to the Israelites at Sinai is proven by the experience of the Israelites themselves. Hundreds of thousands of them literally heard the voice of God. This was a primary, objective event that could not be denied or explained away. We can trust in the truth of that revelation since so many of our ancestors were first-hand participants in it. The historical record of the primary event has been passed down through all the generations.

Hearing the Voice of God

It is one thing to study the revelation; and another to actually experience it. We need to understand more about the primary experience of direct revelation. The Torah is filled with the sound of the voice of God. He speaks to biblical characters and gives them messages and commandments. God talks to the biblical heroes and they respond in a natural way, as though it is quite normal to carry on a conversation with God. Biblical characters seldom express amazement at having received divine communications.

> Abraham and Sarah are old. They feel the deep pain of Sarah's barrenness. Angels appear and tell the couple that they will have a son. The child, Isaac, is born. Some years pass, and Abraham hears a voice: "Take your son, your only son, whom you love, Isaac, and go to the land of Moriah, and offer him there for a burnt offering on one of the mountains which I will tell you of." The message is shocking and terrible, but Abraham offers no words in response. He wakes up early the next morning, takes his son, and leaves on this mysterious journey to an undesignated mountain. Abraham did not doubt that the voice he heard was God's. He was so certain of the reality of God's communication that he was prepared to take the life of his son.

> Moses is a shepherd in Midian. One day, as he is tending his flock, he spots a burning bush. The flames rise but the bush is not consumed. A voice calls out to Moses, telling him to return to Egypt to lead the Israelites to freedom. Moses feels inadequate to the task; yet the voice insists. Moses leaves the tranquility of his life in Midian and goes to Egypt to redeem the children of Israel. Moses never wondered whether the voice was God or simply his own imagination. Having heard the voice, Moses knew the truth.

God's revelations to humans are the point of contact between the eternal reality of God and the time-bound reality of humanity. Why it happens, how it happens—no one can explain with certainty. But human experience shows that it has happened and does happen.

Prophecy

Rabbi Benzion Uziel, in an essay dealing with the phenomenon of prophecy, considers the opinions of various philosophers concerning how people are able to hear God's voice. What was the experience of the Israelites at Sinai or the experience of the prophets? Rabbi Uziel believes that the voice of God is heard "through channels of the senses of sight and hearing, the results of the formations of air in the form of letters, seen by the eye, or as a created voice which the God of the universe created and initiated ..."[1] In effect, God creates within the human the power to receive His communication; and the communication is not heard in the same way that one hears the words or sounds of other humans.

Medical and psychological research has shown that probing certain parts of the human brain can evoke specific responses. A person might begin to taste, smell, hear, see, or feel something not in response to an outside stimulus but to the probings in his brain. Likewise, the prophetic experience may involve hearing God's words not by means of one's external senses, but by God's implanting the words in a person's brain.

Maimonides believed that prophecy was attained only by those who were worthy of it. But Rabbi Uziel argues that prophecy was experienced and can be experienced by anyone whom God chooses, regardless of qualifications. Rabbi Yosef Albo has written that when a prophet is present, prophecy itself can be spread even to individuals who are not ordinarily fit to receive prophecy, just as was the case at the revelation at Sinai, where everyone heard the voice of God. Rabbi Uziel notes that "these words of Rabbi Yosef Albo have a great basis in life, for our eyes see that the presence of a heroic man at the head of his army spreads a spirit of heroism and courage over his troops, even those who are weak in nature and timid in spirit." A prophet has a similar power to spread prophecy over his followers.

The midrash *Tanhuma* (Exodus 1:22) describes the voice of God at Sinai as having emerged when the world was in total silence. The voice seemed to come from every direction and then from heaven. Rabbi Uziel interprets this midrash as teaching that the voice of God at Sinai was unique, not emanating from an organic body, nor even having a specific place as its source.[2] Rather, it was a miraculous voice that filled the entire universe. The midrash teaches that all the voices on earth have echoes, but that the voice of God at Sinai had no echo. It changed into seven voices and into seventy languages and was heard by each individual according to his or her power. The voice was not heard by the ear canals, but was somehow absorbed by the entire beings of the Israelites.

Rabbi Uziel continues:

> Those enlightened ones err who follow the Greek philosopher who says that anything that cannot be understood by reason is not true. To these hardhearted and stupid people we say: have you never heard in your life the voice of God which speaks to you in the hiddenness of the soul? A hidden and secret voice which makes all your limbs tremble and shake? And you are moved by it, and you rejoice from happiness at this voice which guides you and chastises you, which consoles and strengthens, teaches and enlightens, and reveals to you the truth in its clarity in ways which have no evidence in any other way.... Whence comes this hidden voice? And how does it reach your ears and your heart?

Hearing this inner voice is an experience found among all people, each according to one's own intelligence and sensitivity. This experience can give us an inkling into the revelation at Sinai. Though we cannot understand how the revelation was experienced, we cannot doubt its wondrous truth.

> The voice of God heard by our ancestors at the revelation at Sinai returns, and is heard by our ears and our hearts each day through the Torah which goes with us always, to teach us the way of life

in which to walk, and to bring us closer under the wings of the holy Shekhinah of the Holy One of Israel.

The experience of revelation is personal and subjective, yet its truth is so clear that it transcends rational and logical limitations. Each individual experiences revelation differently. This idea has an antecedent in the writings of Rabbi Yitzhak Luria, who taught that there are 600,000 aspects of meaning in the Torah, equal to the number of Israelites who witnessed the revelation at Sinai. The Torah in its fullness cannot be understood unless these 600,000 facets are considered. This idea was also expressed by Rabbi Moshe Cordovero who taught that "each of the 600,000 souls has its own special portion of the Torah, and that to none other than the one whose soul springs from thence, will it be given to understand it in this special and individual way that is reserved to him."[3]

Revelation Versus Religion

Judaism is founded on revelation and prophecy. When God spoke the Ten Commandments to the people of Israel at Sinai, He established a covenant for all time. The sacred texts of Judaism record God's words to our ancestors.

But a paradoxical situation arises. Although revelation and prophecy lie at the foundation of our religious tradition, they are also the most potentially dangerous and unsettling elements within religion. Anyone can claim to have heard the voice of God or to have received a vision from the Almighty. History is studded with an array of false prophets. Even in biblical times it was not easy to distinguish between a genuine prophet and an imposter. Jeremiah debated against false prophets, but he was not believed by many of his coreligionists. Elijah, after having performed a spectacular miracle on Mount Carmel in the presence of a large throng of people, had to flee for his life on the very next day. He prayed to God to allow him to die. Apparently the Israelites were not completely convinced of his divine mission.

Imagine if a father today held a knife to his son's throat. And suppose the father explained that he must sacrifice his son in response to a commandment he received from God. Surely we would do all in our power to stop him, perhaps imagining him to be deranged. Yet Abraham did the same thing in response to the voice he heard, and is judged to be a hero of faith. Who can determine who has actually received a revelation from God and who has not?

Religion, though based on the voice of God, is afraid of the voice of God. An unexpected voice from heaven is disruptive and disorderly. Its very unpredictability is unnerving. A stable and organized community cannot well tolerate individuals who claim to have received a divine communication.

There is an unspoken but real conflict between the spirituality that seeks to hear the voice of God and the religious authority that seeks to maintain orderliness among its people. The two tendencies may maintain an uneasy truce, or they may erupt in conflict. There is a tension between prophets and priests, mystics and rationalists.

The Talmud records a story that is a landmark in Jewish religious history (*Bava Metsia* 59a–b). Rabbi Eliezer and his colleagues (second century CE) became involved in a debate over the ritual purity of an oven owned by someone named Okhnai. Rabbi Eliezer argued that the oven was ritually clean, while the other sages ruled it to be unclean. Since rabbinic law follows the opinion of the majority, Rabbi Eliezer's opinion was overruled. But the rabbi insisted that he was in the right. "If I am correct," he told his colleagues, "let the current of the river outside reverse itself." The current reversed itself. Unimpressed, the rabbis maintained their decision in spite of the miracle. Rabbi Eliezer again challenged: "If I am correct, let the walls of the study hall shake." The walls shook. But the rabbis remained adamant. Finally, Rabbi Eliezer called out: "If I am correct, let a voice from heaven affirm my ruling." A voice from heaven then resounded in approval of Rabbi Eliezer's point of view. But the sages still clung to their decision, retorting that the Torah is "not in heaven." Once God had given the Torah to Israel, He no longer had any authority to intervene in its explication. He had delegated that right to the sages, and it was they who could decide how the law was to be applied. Even when a heavenly voice expresses God's viewpoint, the sages are obliged to follow their own reasoning and not abdicate their responsibility to the divine voice. The law, though based on revelation, is to be maintained by reason.

The Talmudic story relates that shortly after the case of Okhnai's oven, a rabbi met the prophet Elijah and asked him how God had reacted to the rabbis who ignored the heavenly voice. Elijah responded that God was delighted: "My children have been victorious over me," God had stated with pride.

This story, which has had a profound influence on halakhic thought for centuries, indicates that the voice of God is no longer needed or wanted for the resolution of religious questions. On the contrary, religious life is far more organized and predictable when left to human planning.

In line with this attitude is the statement of Maimonides that a prophet has no more authority in Jewish law than any other sage. If a rabbinic court voted on a particular matter and the prophets were all of one opinion while the rabbis were all of the opposite opinion, the law was determined by majority rule. No extra authority is given to the prophets in halakhah.[4]

It is understandable why the sages overruled the power of prophecy. The halakhah could not be left to heavenly voices without undermining rabbinic authority. The law had to be established based on view of the majority of intelligent, rational, and learned rabbis. If a prophet or heavenly voice were allowed to override rabbinical decisions, the law would become too tentative. There would always be the possibility of someone speaking in the name of God that the law was different. It is not divine truth in the absolute sense that is needed for law; it is consensus among the authoritative legislators of the law.

The voice of God did not stop with the decision of Rabbi Eliezer's colleagues. Certainly, the attitude that they manifested did come to prevail in the halakhah. The Talmudic statement that "a sage is greater than a prophet" became an axiom of religious life. But outside the domain of halakhah, individuals were still moved by the voice of God. Jewish tradition also includes the experiences of spiritually elevated people who received divine messages, whose lives were lived in a personal, direct relationship with God.

Messages from Heaven

The city of Safed in northern Israel was a haven for mystics and pietists during the sixteenth century.[5] Many of these religiously inspired people were victims of or children of victims of the expulsion of Jews from Spain in 1492. They came to Israel because it was the Holy Land, the land of prophecy, the land where the messiah would come to redeem the Jewish people.

In the milieu of Safed, individuals longed to hear the voice of God. They attempted to attune their minds and spirits to the heavenly messages that they believed were constantly being transmitted. One of the foremost sages of the Safed community was Rabbi Hayyim Vital, and he described five ways in which a person could obtain divine inspiration.[6] One could be moved by the holy spirit of God Himself, or through the souls of departed saints, or angels known as *maggidim*, or Elijah the prophet, or dreams. Divine messages came to those who were worthy of receiving them and who were receptive to them. Through piety and asceticism, one could come to cling to God and to draw in God's spirit.

Vital indicated a number of preparations that enabled one to receive the holy spirit. These included repentance for all sins; careful observance of all commandments, particularly prayer and love of one's fellow human beings; and purification through ritual immersions and by wearing clean clothes. Finally, he recommended silence and solitude, especially after midnight. Once a person had accomplished these requirements, one should:

> close his eyes, withdraw his mind from all worldly things as
> if his soul had left the body and he was insensible like a dead
> corpse. Thereafter he should make an effort to meditate with
> great passion on a higher world and to cleave there to the roots

of his soul and to the supernal lights. He should imagine in his mind as if his soul has left him and was ascending on high, and he should picture the higher world as if he actually stood there. And if he performs any *yihud,* he should intend thereby to draw the light and the influx down on all the world and also intend to receive his own share in the end.

If in spite of these exercises, one still does not receive illumination from God, it is a sign that one is not yet worthy.

Vital warns that even if an individual attains a prophetic state, the initial illuminations may be uneven and irregular. It will not always be easy to determine whether one is receiving a true revelation or only an illusion of one. Vital observes: "Know that at first the spirit will come upon him as if by accident, on rare occasion only, and also the contents of the revelations will be slight, not profound, and moreover little in quantity. But as he continues his power will increase."

The voice of God could be transmitted through *maggidim,* angelic speakers. There was a belief among mystics that every word uttered by a person leads to the creation of an angel. An individual who is devoted to piety and words of Torah thereby creates many good angels. These angels "are the mystery of the *maggidim,* and everything depends on the measure of one's good works." A *maggid* could manifest itself through automatic speech, its voice coming though the mouth of the person who is to receive the message. Or it could find other ways of making itself heard.

Rabbi Azulai, in his book *Shem Ha-Gedolim,* mentions a number of scholars and rabbis who received messages from *maggidim.* In popular tradition, saintly people were believed to be visited by the prophet Elijah as well as by angels. Divine voices were available to those who had the capacity and saintliness to receive them.

The Case of Rabbi Yosef Karo

The world of supernatural voices and the world of technical halakhic legalism merged in the unusual personality of Rabbi Yosef Karo (1488–1575). Rabbi Karo is best known for his works on Jewish law:

the *Shulhan Arukh*; the *Beit Yosef*, his commentary on Maimonides'
Mishneh Torah; and his responsa. It can be well argued that no other
author in Jewish history has made more notable contributions to
halakhah.

Yet Rabbi Karo also wrote a much less well-known volume, *Maggid
Mesharim*, which is a diary of messages he received from a heavenly
maggid. This book offers an entirely different aspect of the mind of the
author of the *Shulhan Arukh*. The rational halakhist and the mystical
pietist merge in this one man in a remarkable fusion of these two religious tendencies.

While still living in Turkey (early sixteenth century), Yosef Karo
and some of his colleagues met on the eve of Shavuot to spend the
night learning Torah, as was the custom. Among the participants in
that study session was Rabbi Shelomo Alkabets, a noted mystic and
poet. Alkabets described an unusual event that occurred that evening.[7] While Yosef Karo was studying, his mouth suddenly opened
and words emerged, but the voice was not his. Those present watched
and listened in amazement as the voice told them that God approved
of their piety and their dedication to Torah; it also urged them to
leave Turkey to settle in the land of Israel. From this time, the *maggid*
became a regular companion of Rabbi Karo, visiting him often and giving him many instructions.

The *maggid* revealed itself to Rabbi Karo at different times, but
seemed to prefer the hours after midnight or the early morning, especially Shabbat morning. The *maggid* appeared as the embodiment of
the Mishnah, but also represented the divine presence of God. As a
rule, it appeared when Rabbi Karo was alone.

The heavenly voice prodded him to intense piety. In one of its early
messages, it presented a series of instructions: Think only of the Torah
and the commandments at all times. Clear your mind of everything else.
Pray with intense concentration. Do not engage in empty conversation.
Do not laugh. Even if you hear a joke, hold back your laughter and
remain serious. Do not become angry over mundane matters. Do not
eat too much. Refrain from overeating on the Sabbath. Be exceedingly
humble. Always be engaged in repentance. Do not think of women.

The *maggid* promised great things for Yosef Karo. The rabbi was assured that if he constantly thought of the Mishnah and Torah, then "behold, I will make you a prince over my people." The *maggid* promised him fame, universal authority in halakhah, success in his yeshivah (rabbinic academy). The *maggid* advised him to cling always to God, "and you will merit having miracles be performed by you just as they were performed by those who came earlier."

When Rabbi Karo had overslept one Sabbath morning, not having woken up until dawn, the *maggid* chastised him for being lazy. It stated that he would have to improve himself and mend his ways if he wanted further revelations. Yet even as the *maggid* criticized him, it also encouraged him, telling him that he would learn the secrets of the Torah from Elijah the prophet, face-to-face.

In a strange promise, the *maggid* assured Rabbi Karo that he would "be privileged to rise as a burnt offering before me and to be burned for the sanctification of my Name." The idea of martyrdom by burning at the stake for the glory of God was part of the spiritual life of the time, especially in light of the cruelties of the Spanish Inquisition. To a sensitive, kabbalistically inclined person, it was thought to be a tremendous honor to give one's total being to God. Giving up one's physical life for the spiritual life of the afterworld is not a difficult jump in reason.

Interestingly, the *maggid* was primarily concerned with moral guidance and with theoretical kabbalistic concepts. It seldom taught Rabbi Karo halakhah. Nowhere does Rabbi Karo assert authority for his legal works on the basis of the fact that he had received divine guidance. Professor Zvi Werblowsky, in his insightful biography of Rabbi Karo, concluded that "his charismatic or mystical life did not spill over into his daylight activities. The Karo of the codes and the responsa remained healthy, realistic, and down to earth."[8]

But it is not necessary to make a clear dichotomy between the two aspects of Rabbi Karo's personality. In fact, it may be impossible to understand the significance of his legal works without reference to his mystical spiritual life. He longed to hear divine voices and was blessed with a *maggid* who fulfilled this function. Yet everyone cannot merit receiving such personal revelations. For religious Jews, the voice of God is reflected in the Torah and the sacred writings. Halakhah, the way God wants us to live, brings us into a living relationship with the voice of God, even if we cannot hear it directly.

Therefore, Rabbi Karo's legal works are actually attempts to capture and record the voice of God, which has been revealed to the people of Israel from the time of Moses. Whereas the *maggid* is a direct and present voice, the halakhah is a "recording" of a voice which can be replayed again and again. Through the study and observance of the Torah and halakhah, a Jew can put life into the context of God's voice. As one advances in Torah study and observance, one might merit receiving a personal revelation. Legalism and mysticism need not be two disparate entities. They are really interrelated and interdependent. At the root, both are listening anxiously for the voice of God.

The Voice of God Today

In the modern world, it has been unfashionable to listen for the voice of God, to engage in mystical thought and meditation. However, this prevailing rationalism and skepticism tend to strip religion of its soul and meaning. Any religious movement that cannot produce saintly people who truly believe themselves constantly to be in the presence of God is a false and corrosive movement.

Essentially, religion must help one be attuned to the voice of God. This is religion's goal. In Jewish teaching, the voice of God is received through special revelations, through the Torah, and through halakhah. According to rabbinic tradition, the voice of God calls out to us each day. The gift of Jewish spirituality is to listen for this voice.

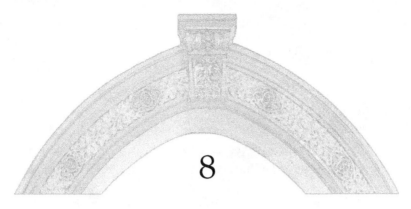

8

TRANSCENDING THE SELF

Think of experiences in your life where you lost your sense of ego, where you transcended yourself and felt part of something greater. Such experiences, which occur to everyone, strike us suddenly, spontaneously. We cannot calculate and prepare ourselves for them. They simply happen to us.

An illustration of this kind of experience is falling in love. Popular language reflects the power of love to overcome us, and we speak of falling in love rather than of directing ourselves into it. The notion of being lovesick goes back at least to the Song of Songs. Someone in love feels a tremendous longing for the beloved.

In his *Dialogues of Love* (sometimes called *The Philosophy of Love*), Judah Abravanel (sixteenth century) writes:

> The proper definition of the perfect love of a man for a woman is:
> the conversion of the lover into the beloved together with a desire
> for the conversion of the beloved into the lover. And when such
> love is equal on both sides, it is defined as a conversion of each
> lover into the other.[1]

Abravanel writes that love is suprarational. It cannot be restrained by reason. In a romantic lament, he describes the state of being in love:

What else can I tell you, save that the lover's part is a continual death in life and life in death? But what I find even more astounding is that, unbearable and overwhelming as is such a lot in its cruelty and tribulations, yet his mind neither hopes nor desires nor designs to escape it, but even holds for his mortal foe whoever counsels or succors him.[2]

There are, of course, other experiences that make us feel that we have gone beyond ourselves, out of ourselves. Sometimes we are particularly moved by music (or other art forms). The music takes hold of us; our hearts jump, our minds drift into it. For those few moments, we experience an ineffable ecstasy. But this experience comes upon us; we cannot plan for it in advance. If we listen to Beethoven's Fifth Symphony in the expectation that we will be powerfully moved, then we are unlikely to be powerfully moved by it. We can only be disappointed, or pretend to be moved. A concert hall might be filled with thousands of people, yet the experience of transcendence, of drifting into the music, may occur only to some of them, for different reasons and in different ways.

There are other occasions when we might feel that we have transcended ourselves. Observing the awesome beauty and grandeur of snow-covered mountains, or a star-filled sky at midnight, or the steady churning of ocean waves—these and other experiences of nature's grandeur can draw us out of ourselves. For a special moment we lose ourselves in the experience, become one with what we are seeing and feeling. For an instant we abandon the concepts of subject and object, feeling rather that we are part of the totality of the experience. There is real and profound unity between ourselves and the world. Such feelings may also occur during prayer or sacred meditation.

Moreover, we might lose our sense of self when caught in the frenzy of a crowd. Our identity merges into the organism of the crowd so that we are swept along within a greater reality than our own private ego. And certainly there are other occasions in life when people experience transcending their egos.

The fulfillment of spiritual life is the feeling of union with God. The moment of religious understanding gives one the sense of having gone beyond oneself. But this religious experience, like falling in love and the other experiences mentioned before, happens of itself. There is no path that, if followed, will automatically lead to this experience of God. The role of religious observance and meditation, therefore, is to provide us with spiritual receptivity, so that we will be ready for the experience when it does come. One cannot force such a religious experience to happen, any more than one can force oneself to fall in love.

Love of God

The Torah teaches a seemingly paradoxical lesson in Deuteronomy 6:5: "And you will love the Lord your God with all your heart, with all your soul and with all your might." This verse is generally taken to be a positive commandment to love God. Yet such a commandment is problematic. Love cannot be commanded. All we can do is prepare ourselves to love and hope that we will indeed love. But if we are required to love, we will face insurmountable obstacles.

The verse in Deuteronomy might be understood not so much as a commandment to love God but as a statement of the consequences of living a spiritually sensitive life. If one observes God's commandments, studies the Torah, teaches the Torah to the children, etc., then it will happen that "you will love the Lord your God with all your heart, with all your soul and with all your might." The result of one's religious preparation and sensitivity will be the blessing of actual love of God with the totality of one's heart, soul, and might.

Jewish mystical tradition has described a framework for spirituality that results in creating receptivity to "fall in love" with God. Jewish mystics developed a variety of techniques to enable themselves to become open to spiritual experience.[3] Among the techniques has been the repetition of particular verses or words, parallel to the use of mantras in Eastern meditation. Kabbalists also involved themselves in writing certain Hebrew words and then permuting the letters in various combinations. Through these and other methods of intense concentration, one stops thinking about the specific words, so that the mind becomes free, open, and receptive. One clears the mind, so to speak, to make room for the religious experience.

Aside from such techniques, kabbalists found value in solitude. Rabbi Elazar Azikri (sixteenth-century Safed) has taught:

> One day a week, a person should distance himself from others and be alone with himself and his Master; he should attach his thoughts to Him as though he is already standing before Him on the day of judgment. He should speak to God, blessed be He, with soft words as a slave speaks to his master and a son to his father.[4]

In another passage, Rabbi Azikri writes that when the pious ones were in solitude, they removed from their minds the matters of this world and attached their thoughts to the Master of all. He recommends that solitude should be practiced once a week, or once in fifteen days, or at least once a month.[5]

Some rabbis in sixteenth-century Safed had the custom of wandering from place to place, almost at random. Rabbi Moshe Cordovero and Rabbi Shelomo Alkabets used to practice this technique. Their conversations were described in a book known as *Sefer Gerushin*.[6] Rabbi Cordovero mentions that on their wanderings they received great insights into the meaning of verses in scripture. These insights came of themselves, without any reflection whatsoever. He stresses the suddenness and spontaneous nature of these insights. "The words of the Torah shined within us and were said of themselves."[7] The wandering served as the technique that heightened receptivity, but the actual experience came of itself.

Jewish mystical thinking has understood that religious observances and meditation serve as the ground from which love of God springs. By creating a thoughtful mood, they help one become receptive to a deep relationship of love with God.

The kabbalists created religious imagery based on experiences in which people transcend their egos—the imagery of falling in love, for example. The Song of Songs, which on the surface appears to be a beautiful example of love poetry between a man and a woman, has been seen at least since the days of Rabbi Akiva as a love story between God and the people of Israel. The very lucid, physical imagery of the Song of Songs is transmuted into spiritual imagery. The underlying message is that one loves God in an analogous fashion to the way a man and woman love each other. Rabbi Cordovero, as well as many others, referred to the community of Israel as the "spouse of the Holy One, blessed be He."[8] The imagery used by mystical thinkers is often quite straightforward. Judah Abravanel has written:

> As we know His perfection, though incapable of apprehending it completely, so we love and desire to enjoy Him in the most perfect union of knowledge possible to us. This great love and desire of ours ravishes us into such contemplation, as exalts our intellect, till, illuminated by special favor of God, it transcends limits of human capacity and speculation, and attains to such union and copulation with God Most High, as proves our intellect to be rather a part of the essence of God, than understanding of merely human form.[9]

One of the beautiful Hebrew poems popularly sung even today is *Yedid Nefesh* by Rabbi Azikri. This poem describes the author's lovesickness for God. His soul longs to be in the presence of God. He refers to God as the "Beloved of the soul." The second stanza begins: "Majestic, Beautiful, Radiance of the universe! My soul is sick for Your love."

Love imagery was also utilized to describe the relationship of Israel and the Sabbath. In Rabbi Shelomo Alkabets' famous poem *Lekha Dodi*, the Sabbath is described as a bride. In fact, this poem has been incorporated into the Friday evening services of Jews throughout the world. We greet the Sabbath with the words, "Come my beloved, to greet the bride; let us receive the face of the Sabbath."

The imagery of love and marriage is highlighted in a number of traditions. For example: it is customary in some communities to recite the Song of Songs prior to the Friday evening service. In this way, the love relationship between God and Israel is placed in the context of the love relationship between Israel and Shabbat. The Talmudic recommendation of marital intercourse on Friday nights has been understood within the mystical tradition as a physical symbol of the spiritual marriage between God and Israel, Shabbat and Israel. Love imagery is particularly noticeable in the prayer books following the custom of Rabbi Yizhak Luria.

Music

The power of music to move and elevate people has been well understood within Jewish religious tradition. The chants and melodies of the synagogue liturgy have a life of their own, quite apart from the meaning of the words that they carry. Some of the most intense and spiritually moving music occurs not in the synagogue, but at the Sabbath meals at home. The *zemirot* (songs) of the Sabbath, sung at the festive Sabbath meals, must be counted among the most powerful emotive forces in Jewish religious life. This music achieves its height among those who are able to give themselves to it without inhibition or self-consciousness.

Many years ago I had occasion to attend a *tish* in Mea She'arim in Jerusalem. The *tish* is a gathering on Friday evening at the synagogue study hall, in which the rebbe—the spiritual leader of the community—presides, and shares of his holiness with the members of his community. I remember that Friday night vividly. I came to the synagogue as an outsider, a Westerner, a doctoral student in an American university. My separateness from the community was manifested in an obvious symbol: I wore a white straw hat, since it was a warm summer evening. Everyone else who wore hats wore black hats. It had to be clear to everyone, even to me, that I was an observer from another civilization, not one of the members of this community.

There was a large table in the room. Sometime before the rebbe arrived, bleachers were placed on either side of the table. Young boys of the community ascended these bleachers and stood on the various benches. The rebbe arrived and went to the head of the table as his followers gathered around in haste. As it happened, I stood at the opposite end of the table from the rebbe so I could see him without impediment; and no one asked me to move. The rebbe donned a prayer shawl and pulled it over his head. The young men on the bleachers started to chant a wordless song. As they sang, the rest of the people in the room began to hum along. The boys closed their eyes and began to sway and rock with their music. The intensity increased, and I felt myself swaying with the rhythm. After a while, the rebbe made a motion and the group stopped singing. His eyes were closed, his facial expression was tight and eager. He put the prayer shawl to his eyes, and I had the impression that he was crying. When he did this, the singing began once again with an incredible intensity. The young men swayed and bowed, their earlocks flying in every direction. As the singing continued, I closed my eyes and tried to let myself join in the spirit of the room. Though I would always be an outsider, I let myself participate in the spiritual life of the community and its music, if only for an instant. But that instant has continued to be important and sacred to me.

Anyone who has allowed herself to enter the spirituality of religious music understands this feeling. Whether it be at a *tish* in Mea She'arim, or at a Friday evening meal at a yeshiva, or in a spiritually alive synagogue, or at the Shabbat table of religiously great people—the power of music to elevate is truly remarkable. It is not surprising, then, that music has played a vital role in Jewish spirituality over the ages.

Prayer

Prayer, whether private or public, is an expression of a human being directed toward God. The words of prayer may express thanksgiving, praise of God, requests for help. Prayers may be uttered spontaneously, or may be repetitions of ancient prayer texts, hallowed by centuries of repetition.

Yet doesn't it seem arrogant for finite human beings to address an infinite and eternal God? What claim can any of us have on God's concern? What right do we have to assume that our lives are so significant that we may ask God to heal us when we are sick, give us strength when we are weak, provide us with all our needs and wants? And how can we find adequate words to express ourselves to God? Inevitably, our words must fall far short of their goal.

And yet we pray. In spite of the above questions, we feel perfectly natural in bringing our petitions, praises, and words of thanksgiving to God. The Bible itself is our precedent. Our ancestors prayed and they were answered. We pray, therefore, not from a rational philosophical justification but from a deeply felt, natural human need.

Prayer is inspired by two different emotions: love and fear. Moses Maimonides has written:

> When a person contemplates His great and wondrous acts and creations, obtaining from them a glimpse of His wisdom which is beyond compare and is infinite, he will promptly love and glorify Him, longing exceedingly to know the great Name of God. As David said: 'My whole being thirsts for God, the living God' (Psalm 42:3). And when he ponders these very subjects, he will be afraid and will recoil, knowing that he is a lowly and obscure creature ... as David said: "As I look up to the Heavens Your fingers made ... what is man that You should be mindful of him? (Psalm 8:4–5). (*Mishneh Torah: Madda* 2:2)

The spiritual context of religion, and therefore of prayer, is dynamic. It fluctuates between feelings of love and feelings of fear, awareness of the spiritual greatness of human beings and awareness of our profound insignificance.

This spiritual tension is an essential feature of Jewish prayer. The morning and evening services both include the recitation of the *Sh'ma*, the classic biblical text affirming the unity and uniqueness of God. The *Sh'ma* is preceded by two other prayers, each of which culminates with a blessing of God. Although the actual texts differ from morning to evening services, and also differ from Sabbath and holidays to weekdays, their themes are identical. The first blessing praises God as Creator, the Almighty Being who oversees the entire universe, whose power is overwhelming. This blessing evokes fear and reverence in us.

We are humbled by our own smallness in relationship to Almighty God. The second blessing, however, focuses on God's love of Israel. It evokes within us a feeling of closeness to God. Its mood contrasts sharply with that of the previous blessings.

After having experienced both moods, fear and love, then the *Sh'ma* is recited, illustrating that God is One. Our contrasting experiences of God, first as the Almighty Creator and then as a loving compassionate God, merge into our greater perception of God's unity. The structure of the prayers leads one to recognize the surprising tension inherent in prayer as well as the surprising satisfaction from unifying dissonant perceptions.

There has always been a tendency for people to develop prayer formulae, in the hope that by our repeating certain magic words, God will do what the worshipper wants Him to do. Prayer of this type is akin to magic. It is particularly appealing to people who tend to be superstitious.

Rabbinic tradition has referred to prayer as "the service of the heart." It transcends the recitation of incantations. Its goal is not to control God, but to give oneself to God. Prayer is the expression of a sensitive and thoughtful soul.

The great kabbalist Rabbi Yizhak Luria taught that it is forbidden to say prayers in sadness.[10] Rather, a person who prays should feel joy, exaltation. Without this joy, the soul lacks the power to receive enlightenment from above by means of prayer. Even when one offers prayers with deep humility, one must retain a great joy at the same time. In listing the laws of prayer, Rabbi Yosef Karo includes the following rules in his *Shulhan Arukh*:

> A person should wait one hour before rising to pray, in order to direct his heart toward God. A person should not rise to pray except with fear and humility; not from the midst of laughter, nor lightheadedness, nor vain matters, nor from the midst of anger. Rather [one should pray] from the midst of joy. (*Orah Hayyim* 93)

An essential feature of prayer is *kavanah*, concentration. In the laws of prayer, the *Shulhan Arukh* also states:

> One who prays must concentrate the heart on the meaning of the words which are uttered from the lips. One should imagine that the Shekhinah is present. One should remove all distracting thoughts until the mind and concentration are pure in prayer … and thus did the pious and saintly people: they meditated and concentrated on their prayers until they reached the level of transcending physicality and elevating the power of the mind until they reached near the level of prophecy." (*Orah Hayyim* 98)

Prayer on its highest level, then, is a devotion of love that unites the worshipper with God. Judah Abravanel, in describing the nature of love, provides a description that very well complements the words of Rabbi Karo concerning prayer. Abravanel writes:

> But when the mind retires within itself to contemplate most earnestly and most closely unite with a beloved subject, it recedes from the external parts of the body, and abandons both sense and movement, gathering to itself for this meditation, the greater part of its faculties and spirits. Only that power is left without which the life of the body could not be maintained: to wit, the vital power, by virtue of which the heart is kept in perpetual motion and the spirits breathe through the arteries.[11]

Prayer on this level is not easy to attain on a regular basis. It should be noted, furthermore, that the spiritual effect of the recitation of prayers is not necessarily tied to the content of the prayers themselves. For example, the recitation of an ancient Hebrew prayer hallowed by centuries of tradition may move the worshipper by the mystery of the words, the melody, the historical association. Translating such a prayer into the vernacular might make its contents more understandable, but at the same time take away the spiritual power of that prayer. For example, the *Kaddish*, chanted in Aramaic by mourners, has a life all its own quite separate from the meaning of its words. Since the *Kaddish* has been recited for centuries by mourners, its deep association with mourning and respect for the dead has a powerful emotive influence on the one who recites it. This is not to advocate that prayers should not be understood for their content. Rather, it is only to say that the meaning and power of a prayer vastly transcend the literal translation of its words.

It is customary in some Jewish communities for pious people to read passages from the *Zohar* as part of their religious lives. The *Zohar* is considered to be a sacred volume, containing the ultimate mysteries and truths of the Kabbalah. Many pious people read the *Zohar*, even without the faintest understanding of the meaning of the words they chant. Yet this very reading imbues them with an overwhelming spirituality and sense of closeness to God. Rabbi Hayyim Yosef David Azulai expressed a wide-spread belief when he wrote,

> The study of the *Zohar* is above any other study, even if one doesn't understand what it says, and even if one errs in the reading. It is a great corrective for the soul. Even though the Torah is composed of the names of God, nevertheless it is clothed in a number of stories. One who reads and understands the stories pays attention to the obvious meaning. But the book of the *Zohar* is composed of the ultimate mysteries themselves, revealed. One who reads them knows that they are the mysteries and secrets of the Torah though they are not understood due to the shortcomings of the perceiver and the profundity of that which is being perceived.[12]

Humility

Through meditation and prayer, a person can transcend the ego. In fact, one's self-awareness may be an obstacle to spirituality. When an artist, for example, becomes self-conscious while creating a work of art, that very self-consciousness creates artificiality and falseness. It is precisely when an artist is so immersed as to lose self-awareness that the artwork is spontaneous and authentic. The ego does not become a barrier between the artist and the art. Likewise in prayer and meditation: it is authentic when it is deep and unifying, when the ego does not intercede between the person and God.

Humility, therefore, is at the root of true spirituality. A humble person is willing to surrender the ego to the religious experience. It may be argued that the many references in the prayer book to our sinfulness are not there to make us feel guilty, but rather to make us aware of our need for humility. The confessions of our sins are not meant to make us feel that we are bad and unworthy, but rather that we ought not be arrogant and egocentric. We should have no qualms at admitting our shortcomings.

Rabbi Bahya ibn Pakuda, a great medieval Sephardic thinker, wrote in his *Duties of the Heart*, that "the primary condition for the service of God is that the worshipper should free himself from the spirit of domination." He noted that a human being's service of God

> can only exist when one assumes all the conditions of servitude—humility and lowliness before God, and rids the self of all forms of domination—grandeur, dignity, haughtiness, self-glory, pride, majesty and any similar feeling.... This service can only be rendered correctly if humility and lowliness before God and submissiveness to Him are genuine; hence it follows that all moral qualities are secondary to humility, which is the head and front of them all. It also logically follows that no moral quality can possibly exist in anyone whose heart is devoid of humility before God or has in it aught of pride, haughtiness or conceit.[13]

Rabbi Moshe Hayyim Luzzatto, in discussing the means of acquiring humility, quotes rabbinic attitudes on humility: "A sign of pride is poverty of Torah (*Sanhedrin* 24a). A sign of complete ignorance is self-praise" (*Zohar Balak*).[14]

Humility can be pretentious, in which case it is not true humility at all. Humility does not mean acting in a subservient and docile fashion; it does mean that a human being is aware of her limitations, of the fact that she is created from dust and will return to dust. This calm wisdom keeps one from taking oneself too seriously. It allows the freedom to transcend insults and petty words of disrespect from others.

Rabbi Moshe Cordovero has taught that a person should learn humility from God Himself.[15] God constantly nourishes everything: even a human being who is sinning against God is sustained by God. God bears the insult and still does good to the one who insults Him. People should emulate this virtue. Be patient. Even if insulted, one should not refuse to bestow goodness. "The quality of humility includes all qualities, for it belongs to the Crown, which is the highest attribute." The Crown always looks down, because it is ashamed to look up at its Source. "So too a person should be ashamed to gaze proudly upwards, but should ever look downwards in order to abase oneself as much as possible."

Rabbi Cordovero states that a person can attain humility, little by little. First, a person should flee honor as much as possible. Second, a person should be aware of his own unworthiness. Third, one should be aware of his sins.

Another way to learn humility is to honor all creatures, recognizing in them the exalted nature of the Creator. Love your fellow human being, even the wicked. Humility means being truly open to the experience of life.

Jewish tradition has drawn on the powerful emotive forces that lead one to transcend the ego: love, music, nature, prayer, and meditation. It has stressed humility as the primary virtue. It was Moses, after all, who was described as the most humble man in the Torah; and it was also Moses who alone saw God "face-to-face."

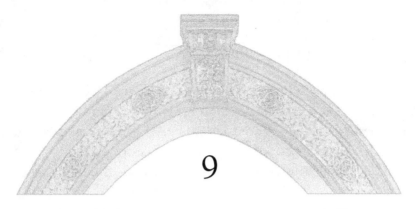

9

PROVIDENCE

The Torah describes God as the Creator of the universe and also as the Being who oversees and is involved in the lives of the biblical characters. God is an active participant in human affairs. He responds to prayers; He reveals Himself to individuals and to the entire people of Israel; He offers rewards and punishments. God is definitely not understood in the Torah as an abstract force or principle.

Jewish spirituality presupposes a providential God. Human beings are not meaningless automatons but are the creations of God. Each person has the possibility of rising spiritually so as to enter a personal relationship with God. Moses Maimonides has posited that the higher one's level of intellectual understanding of God, the more one receives God's providence.[1] But whether or not we accept Maimonides' position, the fact remains that people experience the providence of God in different ways.

One of the persistent problems in religious philosophy deals with the nature of God's providence. Since we like to believe that God is fair and just, why does God sometimes act in ways that seem to be unfair and unjust? Why do innocent people suffer? Why do wicked people prosper? Why does Providence not so manage the affairs of humanity so that the righteous are always rewarded and the wicked always punished? Elements within Jewish tradition underscore the human assumption that God must act justly. For example, when God decided to destroy the wicked citizens of Sodom, He first informed Abraham of His intention. But Abraham offered an objection. Perhaps some righteous people lived in Sodom. Surely God would not destroy the righteous along with the wicked! "Will the Judge of all the world not do justice?" God finally conceded to Abraham's argument and agreed not to destroy the city if even ten righteous people could be found there. The Torah reports that the city was destroyed, but only after Lot and his family (the righteous of the city) were given the chance to escape.

The notion that God must act justly is evident in much rabbinic literature. "The Almighty does not deal despotically with His creatures" (*Avodah Zarah* 3a) is a popular formulation of this assumption.

Yet this pattern does not always seem to be followed in human history. Innocent lives are lost daily; good people are not given opportunities to escape every evil. Our assumption that God is just and merciful often collides with the reality we experience, the evidence of our own eyes.

The Talmud (*Gittin* 56b) records a dramatic confrontation between our assumption and reality. The Second Temple was destroyed by the Roman general Titus. The Talmud relates the horrible deeds of Titus. Jews were slaughtered, sold into slavery, exiled. Titus is characterized as a vicious tyrant, lacking in mercy and respect. The Jews who experienced the destruction of the Temple and the downfall of the Jewish state were in a state of spiritual disarray. It seemed inconceivable that God would allow a cruel, godless Roman to massacre and defeat the Jews, the chosen people of God. Innocent men, women, and children were killed or abused. The suffering was overwhelming.

The Jewish religious response to the catastrophe was imbued with perplexity and anger. Scriptural verses that sang the praise of God were reinterpreted by several rabbis to read as criticisms of God. For example, Psalm 89 extols God and asks, "Who is like You in strength, O God?" Abba Jose ben Hanan interpreted the verse to mean: "Who is like You, so strong and hard, that You hear the curses and blasphemies of that wicked person [Titus] and yet You are silent?" The school of Rabbi Ishmael offered an even more startling piece of exegesis. Exodus 15 includes the verse: "Who is like You among the mighty [*eilim*], O God?" The interpretation is: "Who is like You among mutes [*ilemim*], O God?" God witnessed all the evil that occurred and yet remained silent as innocent blood was spilled. How could He have withheld intervention?

This reaction is paralleled in several elegies composed after the expulsion of Jews from Spain in 1492. One of them begins:

Alas, our Father, is this the recompense
we have sought?
Who is the father who raises children
to take vengeance on them,
to pour anger on them
with great and fuming wrath?
We have sat on the ground, we have also wept.[2]

The poem continues as a dialogue between Israel and God. Israel objects that God had allowed them to suffer so much and so unfairly. God responds that the sufferings are a result of Israel's own sins. Israel retorts: Even if we have sinned, God is supposed to be merciful and forgiving. Moreover, even if some have sinned, can God believe that the children are all so guilty as to deserve such suffering? The dialogue continues until God finally concedes that He will restore Israel, rebuild the Temple in Jerusalem, and fully redeem the Jews. The author of this elegy, which was incorporated in the service for the ninth of Av in many Sephardic communities, insists that God admit His unjustness in His dealings with Israel. God must make recompense for His unfairness.

The above examples reflect anger and incredulity at God's apparent lack of justness. They assume that God must be righteous and must be held responsible for any injustices which occur in the world. They are manifestations of a spiritual double bind, a situation where two opposite truths conflict with each other, leaving us confused and frustrated. One truth is that God is providential, compassionate, and just; the other truth is that many good people suffer, and innocent people die prematurely. There are no evident distinctions between the wicked and the righteous; blessings and curses are distributed among people haphazardly, not because they were earned. Diseases, natural disasters, and genetic defects strike at humans without reference to their righteousness or lack thereof. How do we reconcile our assumptions about God with the realities we see daily in human affairs?

Afterlife

In the *Ethics of the Fathers*, Rabbi Yaacov teaches: "This world is like a vestibule to the future world; prepare yourself in the vestibule so you can enter the banquet hall." By righteous living in this temporal life, one earns eternal life in the world-to-come. The vicissitudes of this life should not be taken out of proportion. No matter how great our suffering may be here, we can look forward to eternal bliss after our earthly death. Rabbi Tarfon has taught (also in the *Ethics of the Fathers*): "Know that the righteous receive their reward in the world-to-come."

These and other similar statements in rabbinic literature try to resolve our human dilemma by stressing the following beliefs: 1) life on earth is temporal and far less significant than the eternal life in the world-to-come; 2) if a righteous person suffers here or if a wicked person prospers, this is only a temporary phenomenon. In the world-to-come, God will reward the righteous and punish the wicked. One should not judge God's ultimate justice by what one sees in this temporal life; one can trust that God's justice will prevail in the next world, which is far more significant than this world.

Rav, a leading rabbi of the third century CE, described the world-to-come as a place free of physical wants and needs. "All that the righteous do is to sit with their crowns on their heads and enjoy the radiance of the Divine Presence" (*Berakhot* 17a). Maimonides believed that the world-to-come is reserved for the righteous and entails pure goodness and eternal life. The reward of the righteous will be to enjoy the splendor of God's presence. The closer one comes to God in this world, the greater will be the spiritual reward in the next world. One who does not live righteously and does not develop intellectual and spiritual abilities will be deprived of sharing the glory of God in the world-to-come.[3]

In stressing the importance of the next world, these sources play down the problems that may arise in this world. Our task is to live properly and to experience our relationship with God as best we can. If we suffer adversity, we should not be deterred from our belief in God's goodness and justice; the rewards and punishments are not generally meted out in this world, but in the next.

Messianism

Yet the Jewish tradition also expresses the belief that God will reward the righteous and punish the wicked even in this world. In messianic times, the righteous will be resurrected from the dead and will enjoy peace and blessing; the wicked will be punished for their sins.

In a broader sense, the messianic idea teaches that Israel will ultimately be vindicated. The many sufferings the Jews have absorbed will be counterbalanced in messianic times by blessings and national freedom. The messianic belief is based on the assumption that history has a direction, that a providential God gives meaning to human events. Professor Gershom Scholem has indicated different tendencies within Jewish messianic thought: a rational view, which sees the messianic era as a natural outgrowth of history; and an apocalyptic view, which sees it as an abrupt, miraculous break with history.[4] The common denominator of these tendencies is that the messianic idea provided the Jewish people with a hope for better times, and a dream of an ideal world that would someday come into being as God's way of demonstrating His justness and fairness to Israel and to humanity as a whole.

The role of the messianic idea in Jewish thought needs to be understood not merely as wishful thinking or nationalistic yearning of the people of Israel. It is not simply a faith for victims, a beautiful dream to pacify a suffering people. Rather, it is a belief in the ultimate justness of God.

Jewish eschatology corrects the distortions of reality as humans experience it. God is certainly just; if things do not appear to verify this truth, then we can be assured that somehow history will vindicate God's justness. If history is filled with injustices, redemption will come to rectify history. Righteousness will be rewarded; evil will be punished.

The messianic idea, then, is not merely the *hope* of the Jewish people, but the *demand* of the Jewish people. God must redeem Israel because Israel has suffered enormously and unfairly. If our eyes do not see God's justness now, we can be sure that the day will come when God's justness is manifest to everyone.

Suffering as a Positive Feature of Life

Suffering in this world can be seen as a positive feature of life. Rabbi Benzion Uziel has written that when we are comfortable and well-off, we tend to ignore God's providential rule of our lives. But when we are suffering, we are brought closer to God.

> Sufferings [*yisurin*] awaken us to examine our deeds, to recognize the righteousness of the justice and the correctness of the judgment; they give us the expression of our lips for prayer and supplication, for thanksgiving and praise to the Creator who created us in justice and who remembers us in justice and who performs kindness for us with justice, with true justice and righteous justice.[5]

Rabbi Uziel argues that it is precisely those who seem to lack the physical blessings of this life who are best able to express deep spiritual feelings. A poor person can pray to God with a pure and full heart, can reach depths of feeling in crying out to God. Likewise, at times of grief or illness a person's spiritual sensitivity is expanded. The sufferings thus lead to a higher spiritual level, a level which would not be reached without adversity.

The Talmudic sage Rabba (some say Rav Hisda) taught: "If a person experiences painful sufferings, one should examine one's conduct. If one can find absolutely no reason to be punished, then one can be sure that these are chastenings of love" (*Berakhot* 5a).

One of the rabbis of the Talmud was known as Nahum Gamzo. The name Gamzo was derived from a Hebrew phrase he always uttered:

gam zo letovah, this also is for the good. His philosophy was that everything that God did was for the best. Since God is perfect, the world
and all that is in it are also perfect. Even things that appear to us as
defects are really good. It is our inadequate understanding that leads us
to think of things as being bad or evil. Our challenge, according to this
way of thinking, is to reconcile ourselves to whatever happens, having
faith that all that occurs is ultimately good because it derives from a
beneficent providence. Suffering should not be experienced as an evil
that God has inflicted on a person arbitrarily, but as an opportunity
for spiritual growth.

The Mystery of God's Ways

Another way of dealing with the problem of evil in the world is to
argue that God's ways are mysterious, beyond our comprehension.
Being eternal, God is not bound in any way by our judgments or our
reason. When Moses asked God for His name, God told him *ehyeh
asher ehyeh,* I am what I am. In other words, God transcends human
understanding.

The book of Job presents an interesting treatment of the problem.
Job, who is righteous, has his faith tested. His children die, his property is destroyed, and he is afflicted with illness. Three friends visit
him and ask him to confess his sins. They believe that it is impossible
for anyone to suffer without deserving the punishment. They believe,
like Abraham in the story of Sodom, that God is a true judge who acts
fairly. Yet Job denies any guilt. He claims that he is suffering although
he has not sinned. But his friends continue to preach to him, torment-
ing him.

At last God intercedes. He answers Job out of the tempest in
chapter 38:

> *Where were you when I laid the earth's foundations?*
> *Tell me, if you know and understand.*
> *Who settled its dimensions?*
> *Surely you should know.*

Who stretched his measuring line over it?
On what do its supporting pillars rest?
Who set its cornerstone in place
when the morning stars sang together
and all the sons of God shouted aloud?
Who watched over the birth of the sea
when it burst in flood from the womb?
When I wrapped it in a blanket of cloud and cradled it in fog,
when I established its bounds, fixing its doors and bars in place ... ?

God describes His enormous power, contrasting it with the powerlessness of human beings. Who controls the weather? Who oversees the lives of the animals? God tells Job:

Brace yourself and stand up like a man.
I will ask questions and you shall answer.
Dare you deny that I am just
or put me in the wrong that you may be right?
Have you an arm like God's arm,
can you thunder with a voice like His ... ?
Look upon the proud man and humble him;
look upon every proud man and bring him low;
throw down the wicked where they stand;
hide them in the dusk together, and shroud them in an unknown
  grave.
Then I in my turn will acknowledge that your own right hand can
  save you.

God's speech is a forceful rebuke to humans. He is beyond our judgments. Humans are powerless and lacking in understanding; compared to the all-powerful and all-knowing God, humans are as nothing. We are in no position to criticize or argue with God. We cannot even begin to understand His ways.

The friends of Job were wrong; God does not punish only as a result of one's sins. Good and evil appear in the world as God chooses, not necessarily as results of human behavior. There is no way we can stand in judgment of God.

The Talmud records a story that elaborates on this theme in *Menahot* 29b. Moses is said to have visited God in heaven and found Him writing a scroll of the Torah. On certain letters, God drew little crowns (*taggin*) and Moses inquired as to their significance. God informed Moses that there would one day be a rabbi so wise that he would understand the entire Torah, each letter and even each crown. Moses was awed and asked for the opportunity to meet this sage. God transported Moses into the future where he found himself in the back of a crowded classroom in which Rabbi Akiva was delivering a discourse in Jewish law. Moses was overwhelmed by the discussion and had difficulty understanding the profound teachings of Rabbi Akiva. When Moses returned to God, he asked: Considering the greatness of Akiva, why did You choose to give the Torah to Israel through me? Akiva is a far better choice. God answered: Be silent; this is My decree.

Moses then asked to see the reward that God had in store for Rabbi Akiva. God again transported Moses into the future, where he witnessed Romans weighing Akiva's flesh in the marketplace after he had been cruelly tortured to death. Moses was stunned. Returning to God, he asked: Is this the reward such a righteous man deserves? God answered: Be silent; this is My decree.

God acts as He acts. He is not subject to our judgment, our approval, or our disapproval. If we do not understand His ways, this is our problem, not His. The Talmudic sage, Rabbi Yannai, admitted, "We cannot explain either the prosperous security of the wicked nor the sufferings of the virtuous" (*Ethics of the Fathers*, 4:19).

Attributing Evil to God

There is an understandable aversion to attributing evil to God. Philosophers such as Maimonides have argued that God does not create evil directly but that evil is simply an absence of good. This is an interesting and subtle philosophic distinction, which is well formulated in *Da'at Tevunot* (*The Knowing Heart*) by Rabbi Moshe Hayyim

Luzzatto. The argument essentially says that God does not create evil. Rather, God created the world through revelation of His spirit and through concealment of His spirit. Not everything shares the same degree of God's spirit. Some are more infused with His spirit, some are less so. Since God, for reasons beyond our understanding, uses direct creation and providence as well as concealment, the continuum of reality has things that are good (more infused with God's direct providence) and things that are less good (toward which God has concealed His presence to some degree). Evil, then, is not an active creation of God, but is a result of God's concealment.[6]

Rabbi Harold Kushner, also unwilling to attribute evil to God, argues that evil happens by itself, and that God has no control to stop it. Kushner believes that it is impossible to believe in a God who created evil and who acts unjustly. Therefore, anything that appears as an evil—diseases, natural disasters, etc.—is not within God's domain but is in the domain of nature, over which God has no control.[7]

Yet the prophet Isaiah had no difficulty in attributing evil to God. He stated candidly that God "forms light and creates darkness; He makes peace and creates evil" (Isaiah 45:7). This verse in Isaiah, in its full candor, contains the seeds of unravelling the problem that we have been discussing. By comprehending the universe as a unity, containing light and darkness, good and evil—all created by God— Isaiah may be removing the problem altogether.

We have been trying to resolve a double bind. We have two contradictory premises: that God is good, fair, just; and that there is evil in the world. We have considered different ways of alleviating the tension of this dilemma. One set of answers assumes that God is just; and the evil is only temporary, or apparent, or it will be balanced by justice in the afterlife and in messianic times. Another set of answers admits that there is evil in the world; and that God can do whatever He likes whether or not His actions win our approval or that God really has no power to stop evil. But none of these answers eliminates the double bind entirely. We are still left with a nagging feeling that the problem is unresolved.

Isaiah's Insight

Isaiah does not attempt to answer our question; rather, he tries to eliminate the double bind that creates our spiritual tension. Perhaps our very question is based on wrong assumptions.

God is One. Everything that exists is a manifestation of God. Light and darkness, life and death, growth and decay—all are part of a unity. They are not in opposition to each other, but are in balance with each other.

The Bible states that God saw the world He created and declared it to be very good. Commenting on Genesis 1:31, Rabbi Moshe ben Nahman relates an ancient Jewish notion that God was pleased that "the order was very properly arranged since the evil is needed for the preservation of the good, just as it is said, To everything there is a season, and a time to every purpose under the heaven." In other words, evil is a necessary feature of the universe; it is a balance for the good.

The first chapter of this book pointed out how deeply attached Jewish spirituality is to the natural world. God reveals Himself through the world He created. The universe inspires within us a recognition of God's power and wisdom. When we observe the natural world carefully, we are awed by its intricacy, its orderliness, its vastness, its might.

But if we study the natural world, we also find things that appear cruel. And we find mutations and defects. These aspects of nature are part of the reality of the universe. They are not mistakes. God has formed the world to include these features, and these features are somehow necessary for the balance of nature.

For example, lions eat zebras. To the zebra being torn apart by a hungry lion, the system does not seem fair. Yet lions must eat zebras as part of the natural order of things. If, out of compassion, we decided to protect zebras from lions, lions would die of starvation and zebras would multiply to an unacceptable level. The natural ecological balance would be upset, plant life would change, food supplies would be altered. An act of seeming compassion would actually be destructive to nature's balance. The eloquent scientist Lewis Thomas has written quite convincingly that nature has its own wisdom, its own set of checks and balances.[8] We may have compassion for the zebra being eaten by the lion, but we know without a doubt that zebras must be eaten by lions. We may feel grief at the death of an individual person, but we know that everyone must die. We can observe the ways of nature, even though we cannot necessarily explain why the balances are as they are.

The universe contains peace and harmony, but also eruptions and disharmony. Both dimensions are part of the same reality and are part of God's creation. They cannot be understood separately but only in relationship to each other.

Nature has its own system of operation. Within the system are things that cause pain and death. Nature does not distinguish between good people and bad people; all are equally subject to bacteria, earthquakes, crippling diseases. Though no one may choose to be a victim of the "evils" of nature, everyone knows that these are part of nature and that people will inevitably be stricken. Most people will admit this, but will also admit that they would prefer for these things to happen to someone other than themselves and their loved ones.

The question is not one of good and evil. Nature is neutral. Even the Bible recognizes that nature has its laws and that God does not tamper with them except in extraordinary cases known as miracles. No one can depend on divine intervention to counteract the flow of nature. Normally, nature carries out its set of balances; no one can tamper with these balances without bringing on a whole new set of problems.

Good and evil are not objective realities, but are interpretations that we give to things. When we say that something is good or bad, we are really saying that our opinion of that thing is good or bad. The forces of nature as created by God are neutral; depending on how one is affected by these forces, one will say something is good or something is evil.

For example, suffering is to a large extent determined by the individual who is undergoing the suffering. Outside observers cannot know the truth of the situation but can only project their own feelings. Being in pain may not be considered evil to the person having the pain. Marathon runners often find themselves in tremendous pain, but this does not evoke self-pity or spiritual struggle. On the contrary, the pain is part of a glorious experience. An observer, watching the runner hobbling toward the finish line, may express pity for the poor runner who is in such agony. But the runner may be filled with inexpressible joy in spite of physical discomfort—joy that the observer may not even imagine.

A more dramatic example may be drawn from children with Down's syndrome. Outsiders may display pity or sympathy for these children, viewing them as unfortunate victims. They may ask why God created defective individuals. Yet within the minds of the children themselves there may be no self-pity or anger at God. Within their own minds, they may be the happiest children on earth. They are delighted with the slightest progress they make, they are affectionate and cheerful. Can an outsider fairly judge their true condition and satisfaction with life and with the God who created them?

We arrive at the following conclusions:

1. God has created the universe, with all its features.
2. Things that appear to us to be good or evil are our own perceptions, not objective descriptions of reality.
3. The natural world that God created is neutral, making no distinctions based on the righteousness or wickedness of people.
4. God can defy the laws of nature, in a miraculous way, but does so very seldom, and certainly no one has a right to expect miracles.

The Talmud (*Hagigah* 14b) tells a story of four rabbis who entered the *pardes*, the sphere of metaphysical speculation. They wanted to understand God's ways, to deal with the double bind of a good God doing evil. One of the sages died. One lost his mind. Obviously, the problem was too powerful for them. Rabbi Elisha ben Abuyah became a heretic; he concluded that "there is no justice and no Judge." The double bind could not be resolved, so he gave up his assumption of a just God.

Rabbi Akiva, though, entered the *pardes* in peace and left in peace. Confronted by the same double bind as the others, Akiva was yet able to live in peace with his faith. He realized that the problem itself was based on wrong assumptions, that the universe is a harmonious unity, that the things we call good and bad are subjective judgments. He recognized the wisdom of Isaiah's statement that God created good and evil, light and darkness—that the balance of the world depends on these forces. They are not mutually exclusive but exist in a necessary relationship with each other. If there were no darkness, light would have no meaning. If there were no death, life would have no meaning. If there were no evil, good would have no meaning. We may not particularly enjoy it when the "evil" elements of the universe are victimizing us or those we love, but we cannot help but realize that these elements are necessary parts of the universe.

Humans do not have a comprehensive view of the universe. We are mortal and finite. God, being beyond time and space, encompasses the mystical unity of the universe. His perspective is complete. Lewis Thomas has offered a significant insight, which serves to underscore the difference in comprehending the universe between God and humans:

> The individual parts played by other instrumentalists—crickets or earthworms, for instance—may not have the sound of music by themselves, but we hear them out of context. If we could listen to them all at once, fully orchestrated in their immense ensemble, we might become aware of the counterpoint, the balance of tones and timbres and harmonics, the sonorities. The recorded songs of the humpback whale, filled with tensions and resolutions, ambiguities and illusions, incomplete, can be listened to as a part of music, like an isolated section of an orchestra. If we had better hearing, and could discern the descants of seabirds, the rhythmical tympani of schools of mollusks, or even the distant harmonics of midges hanging over meadows in the sun, the combined sound might lift us off our feet.[9]

What we perceive in fragments, God encompasses in toto. It is an awesome and humbling thought.

Human Evil

Many of the evils that humans complain about are actually created directly by humans, not by God. Violent crimes, wars, air pollution, water contamination, transportation accidents, etc.—all are the result of human freedom. Yes, God implanted in humans the capacity for doing good and evil, and perhaps even gave evil a bit more sway in the human species. But humans have the freedom to choose to do what is good, kind, and compassionate. If they choose to murder, rape, and plunder, their evils should not be attributed to God.

The Nazi Holocaust has caused considerable spiritual unrest among Jews in the twentieth and twenty-first centuries. It seems incomprehensible that millions of innocent Jews should have been so methodically and savagely murdered by the Germans and their allies. People ask: Where was God? Why did God not intervene? How could God have allowed innocent people to fall victim to cruel and wicked people? How can we hope to understand the tragedy of the destruction of one and a half million children by the Nazis?

And yet these questions are not properly addressed to God but to humans. God did not create the war. He did not create Nazi ideology, or instill viciousness in them, or build their gas chambers, or load their guns. The most horrible thing about the Holocaust was that it was entirely a human creation. It was started by humans, maintained by humans, and was not stopped by humans who should have opposed its horrors.

The Holocaust should inspire us with disgust, anger, and even despair—emotions directed against humans for being capable of such heinous crimes and for allowing such savagery to take place. We cannot in any fairness blame God for the Holocaust.

But we are bothered by the fact that God remained silent while innocent people were being slaughtered by the millions. We are angry that He did not perform some miracle to change the course of events. But we have no right to expect miracles; life follows its own course, and dramatic miracles seldom intervene. That is not God's problem; it is our problem. We need to rely on ourselves, on human resources.

A rabbinic legend teaches that when the Temple in Jerusalem was being razed by the Romans, the Jews were amazed that God could have allowed this to happen. They thought that in recognition of this terrible tragedy the sun should have grown dim. But the sun glowed as usual, giving no indication at all that the natural world shared in the sadness of Israel. God taught them that He placed the natural world in its set order and that it would carry out its laws. No one could expect these laws to change, in spite of the vicissitudes of human events.[10]

The Chosenness of Israel

Although natural laws prevail and human affairs are largely left to humans, God's providence does manifest itself in the lives of individuals and in the lives of nations. God's providence is evidenced in His covenant with Israel. God revealed Himself to the Israelites and gave them the Torah as a guide for their lives. The Torah speaks of Israel as a chosen people; this chosenness is itself an indication of God's involvement in the affairs of humans.

That Israel has been selected by God for a unique destiny is clear; this chosenness becomes more obvious with the passage of time. The ancient Israelites received the Torah, were given prophets, and created a religious literature that has dramatically influenced the course of human history. The Jews have carried the Torah and its teachings through the millennia, in many different lands, often under severe oppression and persecution. Yet the Torah still affects human life today, and the Jews are still here as living witnesses of God's covenant with ancient Israel. The special nature of Israel's relationship with God is understood best through history, not through philosophic speculation.

Rabbi Yehuda Halevy, in his *Kuzari*, has also expressed the idea that God's providence toward Israel is best evidenced in history.[11] The *Kuzari* is a literary creation based on a historical foundation. The king of the Khazars felt the need to follow the true religion. Ultimately he and many of his people converted to Judaism. Halevy composed dialogues between the king and sages representing philosophy, Islam, and Christianity. The king was dissatisfied with all of them. Finally he called a Jewish sage and asked about his belief.

> The rabbi replied: "I believe in the God of Abraham, Isaac, and Israel, who led the children of Israel out of Egypt with signs and miracles; who fed them in the desert and gave them the land, after having made them traverse the sea and the Jordan in a miraculous way; who sent Moses with His law, and subsequently thousands of prophets, who confirmed His law by promises to the observant, and threats to the disobedient. Our belief is comprised in the Torah—a very large domain."
>
> The king objected to this answer. "Now, O Jew, shouldn't you have said that you believed in the Creator of the world, its governor and guide, and in Him who created and keeps you, and such attributes which serve as evidence for every believer, and for the sake of which he pursues justice in order to resemble the Creator in His wisdom and justice?"
>
> To this the rabbi responded: "That which you do express is religion based on speculation and system, the research of thought, but open to many doubts. Now ask the philosophers, and you will find that they do not agree on one action or on one principle, since some doctrines can be established by arguments, which are only partially satisfactory, and still much less capable of being proved."

The conversation continued and the rabbi later offered a parable. If you were told that the king of India was a great man, just, admirable, virtuous, and a wonderful leader of his people, would this information cause you to revere him? The answer must be no, since you cannot judge the truth of these statements in the abstract. However, if the king sent you gifts that reflected his wisdom and generosity, compassion, etc., would you be able to make a better judgment about him? The answer is yes. So too it is with God. Statements about his attributes are philosophical abstractions, and cannot be verified on their own terms. When we want to know about God, we need to evaluate the gifts He has given us—the universe, the Torah, our lives. From these creations we can proceed to understand aspects of God. It is experience—history—that is the source of our understanding of God. It is our ancestors who have passed down to us their own experiences with God and who have shown us how God has manifested Himself to them in their lives. It is beyond human ability to describe how God's providence works in every detail. It is not fair to attribute each success or failure, each day of health or illness to a specific decision of God to reward or punish someone. We lack control and understanding of God's providence. God told Moses: I am what I am. Yet this incomprehensible God has also revealed Himself to human beings through the universe He created, and to Israel, through the Torah, which He has given this chosen people.

It is One God who creates light and darkness, good and evil. To understand this reality, human reason is inadequate. The truth is to be sought in personal spiritual experience, in profound meditation and calm.

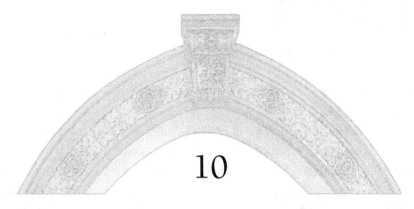

10

CONFRONTING DEATH

Is Death a Problem?

In our modern society, death is an evil to be postponed or camouflaged. In its aversion to death, our culture teaches us even to avoid saying that someone has died. Rather, we substitute euphemisms such as "passed away" or "passed on" or "expired."

Since the aging process is identified with the approaching of death, aging is also viewed as a problem. Billions of dollars are spent each year on cosmetics, dyes, medical procedures, and other vanities—all in an effort to hide the aging process.

Clearly death is a problem for our society. Doctors are supposed to cure our diseases and prolong our lives indefinitely. In some way, death may be seen as a failure of medical science. If only the right drugs could be discovered; if only a new operation could be perfected; if only more research could be financed ... then, presumably, we would not have to die, or at least not for a very long time.

Elias Canetti, in his book *The Torch in My Ear*, has expressed the modern repugnance for death:

> The aim is not to parrot the banality that so far all human beings
> have died: the point is to decide whether to *accept* death willingly
> or stand up against it. With my indignation against death, I have
> acquired a right to glory, wealth, misery, and despair of all experi-
> ence. I have lived in this endless rebellion.[1]

This is a point of view that appeals to our sense of heroism, our intellectual existentialism.

Ernest Becker's *The Denial of Death* is built on the modern assumption that death is at the root of human fear and is the underlying motivation of our patterns of behavior: "The human animal is characterized by two great fears that other animals are protected from: the fear of life and the fear of death."[2] Death creates terror within us, and this terror dominates our lives.

Philippe Aries, who has studied Western attitudes on death over the centuries, notes that in earlier times the terror of death was not as pronounced as it is now. In fact, he suggests that the oldest kind of death is the "tame death," the death that is accepted in a fairly natural, non-fearful way:

> It has by now been so obliterated from our culture that it is hard for us to imagine or understand it. The ancient attitude in which death is close and familiar yet diminished and desensitized is too different from our own view, in which it is so terrifying that we no longer dare say its name.[3]

For moderns in the Western world, although we may verbalize that death is natural and normal, we rebel against this knowledge. We idealize heroes who defy death or who scorn death—even if they themselves die in the process. This is one of the ironies of human existence: our prize for running the obstacle course of life successfully is to die of old age.

Death Defiance

Franz Borkenau has characterized cultures as death denying (such as modern America), death accepting (such as Eastern civilizations), or death defying (such as among warlike peoples).[4] Obviously cultures contain elements of all these characterizations and can never be neatly confined to the definitions of psychologists and anthropologists. Yet these are useful categories that generalize dominant tendencies within societies. Rabbi Maurice Lamm, author of *The Jewish Way in Death and Mourning*, gave a lecture in which he described the Jewish attitude as being death defying.[5] Jewish tradition has emphasized the sanctity of life, the obligation to preserve life even when it entails violating halakhah. One may desecrate the Sabbath to save a life; one may eat forbidden food if that is the only way to save a life. The intent of halakhah is clearly to support life and to preserve its sanctity. When life is endangered, the halakhah is to violate halakhah if that can lead to the saving of a person's life. In its desire to defy death, Jewish tradition does everything possible to insure a continuance of life.

The Jewish attitude is reflected in the confession that one is supposed to recite before dying. The *Shulhan Arukh* records the text of the confession:

> I admit before You, God, my God and God of my ancestors, that my cure and my death are in Your hands. May it be Your will that You heal me with a complete healing. And if I die, may my death be an atonement for the sins, transgressions and violations which I have sinned, transgressed and violated before You. And place my portion in the Garden of Eden, and let me merit the world-to-come reserved for the righteous. (*Yoreh Deah* 338:2)

The confession indicates a tenacity to hold on to life. Even when it appears obvious that one will die, one first asks God for healing. Only then does the individual consider the eventuality of death. The confession is conditional, not admitting the inevitability of death.

Jewish legal sources emphasize the responsibility of helping the ill person in the battle against death. For example, the *Shulhan Arukh* rules that it is forbidden to tell a seriously ill person of the death of a close relative (*Yoreh Deah* 337). Such news could break one's heart and reduce the ability to resist sickness. Even if a relative died over whom the ill person is obligated to mourn, we are still not to inform that person of the death, nor cry, nor eulogize in the person's presence. Rabbi Yoel Sirkes, in his commentary known as the *Bah*, comments that we should not even inform an ill person of the death of a non-relative. By our mention of someone else's death and by our display of sadness, the ill person may become frightened and disheartened.

When informing a dying person of the obligation to recite the confession, we must do so in a cautious and gentle way. The halakhah provides a formula: "Many have confessed but have not died; and many who have not confessed have died. And many who are walking outside in the marketplace confess. By the merit of your confessing, you live. And all who confess have a place in the world-to-come." Rabbi Sirkes suggests that an ill person should not be told to confess unless obviously in the process of dying. But if one is not yet at that last stage, one should not be told to confess, even in a gentle fashion, since this would break the heart and make one give up the fight for life.

The reverence for life over death is also evident in the laws concerning a *goses*, a dying person in the last hours of life. The halakhah prescribes that a *goses* should not be moved, since even the slightest disturbance might cause death. Someone who does move a *goses* is equated with one who has shed blood. The message is emphatic: death must not be hastened; life is sacred.

The Jewish laws of mourning seem to view death as a defeat. Mourners tear their garments, and for seven days they sit on the floor, refraining from shaving or wearing new or cleaned clothes. They do not wear leather shoes, and they avoid social conversational amenities. These are all signs that death is bad. Death angers and frustrates us.

Jewish defiance of death is illustrated by some prophetic verses that are recited during the mourning period. Drawing on the words of Isaiah, we console the mourners by saying that

[God] will utterly destroy death forever;
and the Lord God will wipe the tear from every face....
Your dead shall live again, the mortal being shall rise up;
awake and sing joyously, you who dwell in the dust,
for as the reviving dew on grass shall be your dew,
when earth shall bring forth her dead.

Ultimately, then, death will itself be defeated by God, and life will prevail. Belief in the resurrection of the dead and in the "destruction" of death certainly contribute to the idea that Jewish culture is death defying.

Death Acceptance in Jewish Tradition

It is inaccurate, however, to define Judaism as being a death-defying culture. There are also strong elements—even dominant elements—that show Judaism to be accepting of death. Too seldom is attention given to the death-accepting aspect of Jewish religious culture.

Which of the biblical heroes in the Torah expresses a fear or dislike of death? Where do our biblical ancestors express a defiance of death? The fact is that they lived quite at ease with the idea of dying. The Torah relates that when Abraham died, he was old and satisfied, and that he was gathered unto his ancestors. On reading about Abraham's death, we are not saddened, nor do we feel that Abraham himself was sad. Rabbi Moshe ben Nahman noted about Abraham's death that God shows the righteous people the reward they will receive in the world-to-come.[6] This information satisfies the righteous as they are dying. This means that the righteous, such as Abraham, do not resist their impending death; they welcome it.

This pattern continues throughout the Torah. When Isaac was old and expected to die, he planned to give his blessing to his son. When Jacob neared death, he called Joseph to ask him to arrange his burial in the land of Canaan. He then gave his blessing to his grandsons, and also left his last words to his children. Isaac and Jacob seem to have accepted the reality of death and tried to put their houses in order before dying. There is no evidence of death defiance.

Before Joseph died, he candidly told his brothers that his end was near. He told them that God would one day lead the children of Israel back to the Promised Land. He also left instructions that his bones should be brought out from Egypt when the Israelites ultimately returned to their own land.

The Torah offers a description of the death of Aaron the high priest. God informed Moses and Aaron that Aaron would be gathered unto his people (Numbers 20:22–29). Aaron's priestly garments were removed and given to his son Elazar. A midrash teaches that Moses did not inform the Israelites of Aaron's approaching death.[7] He feared that, since they loved Aaron so much, they would pray to God to spare Aaron's life, attempting to prevent God's decree from being fulfilled. But this would be contrary to God's wise plan; Aaron was supposed to die. Death was not an evil for him.

Even the death of Moses is consistent with the pattern of death acceptance. Moses did not ask for immortality, only for the privilege of living long enough to enter the Promised Land. The tragic quality of his demise is not due to the fact that he died, but that he died without having fulfilled his goal.

Accepting death as the natural end of life does not imply that life is unimportant or not worth preserving and extending. Biblical characters accepted the reality of death, but did not want to die violently or prematurely. Cain, Lot, and Jacob all expressed fear of dying in an unexpected or violent way. But this does not mean that they defied death once their natural end had come.

There are many evidences in rabbinic literature that also reflect death acceptance. A midrash informs us that when Sarah died, Abraham and all the people of the land mourned for her. The weeping and lamenting were so universal that Abraham himself had to offer consolation to others. "My children," he said, "take not the death of Sarah too much to heart. There is one event unto all, to the pious and impious alike. I pray you now, give me a burying place with you, not as a gift but for money."[8] Philo wrote that Abraham mourned only a short time for Sarah, since immoderate mourning would be unfitting for a wise person, who should not feel sorry when restoring to God the deposit entrusted to Him (De Abrahamo 44).

The same idea finds expression in the story of the students of Rabbi Yohanan ben Zakkai, who came to console their master on the death of his son (Avot de Rabbi Natan, chapter 14). Only Rabbi Eliezer ben Arakh gave proper consolation. He said:

I will give you a parable to what the matter should be compared: to a man who was given an object to watch by the King. Each day he would cry and scream. He would say: 'Woe unto me! When will I peacefully be free of this object?' So it is with you, Rabbi. You had a son who learned Torah, prophets and writings, mishnah, halakhot, aggadot, and he has been freed from this world without sin. Shall you receive consolations when you have returned intact the object entrusted to you?

The Talmud reports that King David sang a special song (*shirah*) five times: in his mother's womb; when he was born and saw the stars; when he was nursed by his mother; when he saw the wicked destroyed; and, finally, he sang a song when he considered the day of death (*Berakhot* 10a). What song did he sing? "*Barekhi nafshi,* bless the Lord, O my soul. Lord my God, you are very great, you are robed with glory and majesty."

A striking midrash remarks that the day of Adam's death was celebrated by his descendants as a festival (*Eliyahu Rabbah* 16:81). They rejoiced that man is mortal, for otherwise he would not do the will of his heavenly Father. Death is not accepted with passive resignation, but with song and festivity.

That death is considered to be an actual good is reflected in the midrash on Genesis 1:31. The Torah states that when God finished creating the world, He looked at it and declared it to be very good. The midrash (*B'reishit Rabbah*) interprets the words "behold it was very good" as referring to death. That is, God examined His creation, realized that death was a feature of it, and declared that the creation was excellent. Without death, the world would be imperfect.

The ultimate meaning of human life is inextricably bound to the fact that humans die. Mortality provides life with intensity, deep emotion, and profundity. To deny or to defy death is to deny or defy a primary source of life's meaning.

Rabbi David ibn Abi Zimra, one of the great Sephardic rabbis of the sixteenth century, considered the following question: how could Adam have followed Eve's advice to sin after he had been so well treated by

God?[9] He answered: It is well understood that everything ultimately returns to its origin. This is true of all living things including humans. Adam knew this. When God commanded Adam not to eat from the tree of knowledge of good and evil, He threatened the punishment of death. This referred to an essential death, not a natural death. Adam realized that his natural death was inevitable; he did not believe himself to be immortal. Adam knew that there was a tree of life in the Garden of Eden but did not know where it was. The snake's argument to Eve, later conveyed by Eve to Adam, was that if they ate from the tree of knowledge of good and evil, they would be like God in their knowledge and understanding. Adam believed that if he ate from the tree of knowledge he would learn where the tree of life was. He could then eat from it and serve God eternally, without fear of death. He reasoned that it would be satisfactory to transgress one of God's commandments in order to gain the privilege of serving God forever. This explains Adam's motive for violating God's commandment. But he was punished because his premise was wrong. God did not want him, or other humans, to be immortal like the angels. He wanted death to be part of the human condition.

A death-defying culture is troubled by death. A death-accepting culture is at ease with the idea of dying. The Jewish tradition is a balance between these two types of culture. The death-defying elements of Judaism heighten concern for the value of life. The death-accepting aspects teach one to face death with wisdom and realism. Understanding how to die gives us understanding for how to live.

The Talmud records a statement by Rabbi Yohanan who, when finishing his study of the book of Job, said:

> The end of a human is to die and the end of an animal is to be slaughtered and everything stands ready for death. Happy is the one who was raised in the Torah and whose involvement was in the Torah; such a one brings pleasure to the Creator. Such a one was raised with a good name and died with a good name from this world. About such a one, Solomon said: 'Better is a name than precious oil, and the day of death than the day of birth.'" (*Berakhot* 17a)

Rabbi Yohanan offers a classic Jewish perspective on death and life. Death is natural and inevitable; but this does not mean that life is merely a dream, an illusion without meaning. Rather, one should live a life dedicated to Torah and earn a good name. The day of death is better than the day of birth in the sense that the struggle through life has been completed. Looking back at a total life, it is possible to evaluate if it was lived well, in accordance with the teachings of the Torah. Death is accepted with wisdom, not despair.

Death from the Perspective of the One Who Is Dying

Discussing and contemplating death as outside observers is different from dealing with death while actually undergoing the experience of dying. There is important wisdom to be culled from those who face death experientially, not merely as an intellectual abstraction.

Dr. Elisabeth Kübler-Ross, in her research with terminally ill people, has concluded that the dying person passes through different stages in dealing with illness and ultimately death.[10] One may deny the illness or may visit one doctor after another hoping for a favorable diagnosis. One may hide the illness from friends and family. A dying patient will enter a stage of anger: *Why me?* This may lead to bargaining with God for an extension of life, promising to be a better person if recovery is granted. Finally, one will face practical issues of setting one's house in order, making sure one's will is drawn up, and that all unfinished business is settled.

When a person realizes that she is really dying, she may sink into a state of depression and begin to mourn the impending death. She may withdraw into silence, showing little interest in those who visit. Finally, once having passed through these stages, she will arrive at acceptance of death. At this stage, she is beyond grief and sorrow, beyond depression and sadness. With acceptance, the person has reached the point of being ready to die, and even wants to die.

This point of acceptance is a pleasing climax to life. One has attained life's most profound wisdom, seeing life for what it is, without illusion or delusion. Lewis Thomas has written, "We may be about to redis-cover that dying is not such a bad thing to do after all. Sir William Osier took this view: he disapproved of people who spoke of the agony of death, maintaining that there was no such thing." Drawing on the research on people who seemed to die but then were resuscitated, Thomas notes that "those who remember parts or all of their episodes do not recall any fear or anguish. Several people who remained con-scious throughout, while appearing to have been quite dead, could only describe a remarkable sensation of detachment."[11]

A Jewish perspective on the experience of death is offered by Rabbi Haim David Halevy, late Sephardic Chief Rabbi of Tel-Aviv.[12] Drawing on recent scientific research, as well as on Jewish mystical texts that describe the experience of death, Rabbi Halevy concludes that death is actually a marvelous happening. It is filled with light, glory, satisfac-tion. Interviews by psychologists of people who have seemingly died but then returned to life indicate that these individuals experienced death uniformly as a wonderful thing.

Death, then, is not experienced by the dying person as something bad. If a person is ready for death, it may indeed be a beautiful event. A Talmudic aphorism teaches, "One who dies in the midst of laugh-ter—this is a good sign. One who dies in the midst of crying—this is a bad sign" (Ketubot 103b). Death acceptance brings a happy death. Death resistance brings tears and suffering.

Reaching a level of death acceptance may be the most profound experience a person can have in life. One can view life from the per-spective of one who is about to leave this world. One who is dying, and who accepts this reality, may attain new insight and understand-ing; it is as though one receives the key to solving the riddle of life. Attaining death acceptance before dying is a blessing of serenity, wis-dom, and love.

Considering death from the perspective of the dying leads to an appreciation of the wisdom of Jewish tradition, which views death as tov me'od, very good. Since we value life, life should be respected and maintained. But since we also value death, it should be accepted when it comes.

The Talmud records questions that Alexander of Macedon asked to a group of rabbis (*Tamid* 32a). Two of the questions and the rabbis' responses are: Question: What should a person do in order to live? Answer: He should make himself die. Question: What should a person do in order to die? Answer: He should make himself live.

This enigmatic dialogue might be understood as follows:

What should a person do in order to live? He should be aware of his own impending death, imagining himself to be dying. In this way, he will appreciate the value of every moment of life. He will see things with an intensity and love that can only be experienced by someone who appreciates that he is about to lose something precious. In other words, in order to live meaningfully, one must recognize one's own mortality.

What should a person do in order to die? He should make himself live. He should live his life fully, without fear of death. He should avoid becoming melancholy over the reality of death. If one gives herself fully to life, she can give herself fully to death when the time comes.

Mourning

If death is good and is to be accepted as a positive feature of God's creation, why do we mourn our dead? Why are funerals so somber? Why is death associated with crying, wailing, and lamenting?

These questions return us to the balance that the Jewish tradition strikes between death defiance and death acceptance. So much emphasis is placed on life that death is not easy to accept. Yet wisdom is to accept death. Rabbi Yaacov taught: "Better is one hour in penitence and good deeds in this world than all the life of the world-to-come; but better is one hour of spiritual repose in the world-to-come than all the life of this world" (*Ethics of the Fathers* 4:22). There is an ambivalence, a recognition of the balancing values of life and death.

Philosophically speaking, we probably should not mourn for our dead. In fact, we probably do not mourn for them even when we think we do. According to Jewish tradition, the soul is immortal. A person who has died—certainly a good person—will receive magnificent rewards from God in the world-to-come. Moreover, the one who has died is now free from all the turmoil, pain, and confusion of this world. No, we do not cry for the one who has died. We cry for ourselves. We mourn because we will miss the presence of the loved one who has died. We feel lonely, deprived, perhaps even guilty for our bad behavior toward the deceased. We mourn because we feel sorry for ourselves. These are legitimate feelings. Even though we might affirm philosophically that death is a positive feature of creation, we are still pained by the loss of a loved one. Philosophy is one thing; emotional reaction is quite another. And both elements must balance each other. Jewish tradition requires us to mourn our near relatives—even if we have philosophically accepted death. But Jewish tradition forbids us from mourning over much, since we must recognize death as part of God's design.

The Jewish laws of mourning balance emotionalism and philosophical wisdom. Mourners are supposed to cry and are expected to participate in burying the dead. There is no camouflage of death, no attempt to deny the starkness of what has happened. Mourners tear their garments, sit on the floor for seven days, and withdraw from their normal social context. They are free to be angry, upset, guilt-ridden. But mourning is not just a private matter. During the seven-day mourning period, friends and relatives visit the mourners and offer consolation. In fact, the mourners, who ostensibly want privacy in order to grieve over their loss, are placed into an active social setting. They see friends and relatives whom they may not have seen for a long time. People come with kind words, gifts of food, warm reminiscences. Even as the mourners feel a desire to be alone in their sadness, they also feel drawn to the well-wishers who come to share the experience with them.

The blend of Jewish wisdom and Jewish realism is apparent in a Talmudic discussion that deals with the question of what people should say when they come to a house of mourning (*Berakhot* 46b). The opinion of the sages is that they should say the blessing *barukh hatov ve-hameitivt*, blessed is God who is good and who does good. Rabbi Akiva disagrees, saying that they should recite the blessing *barukh dayan ha'emet*, blessed be the true Judge. The opinion of the sages seems to be that death must be accepted as a positive good; therefore, we recite a blessing praising God's goodness when visiting a house of mourning. Rabbi Akiva, on the other hand, suggests a blessing that expresses resignation in the face of death. The Talmudic discussion concludes that both blessings are to be recited. In fact, the themes of both blessings are incorporated in the blessing following the mourner's meal after a funeral. The text is:

> *You are good and You do what is good.*
> *You are the God of truth and Your decree is just.*
> *You take back our souls in Your universal rule, doing according to*
> * Your will,*
> *and we are Your people, Your servants.*
> *Whatever befalls, we must acknowledge You and bless You.*

After making these statements recognizing God's goodness and justness, the text goes on:

> *May He who gives strength to the bereaved*
> *in His compassion give solace in this bereavement to us and all His*
> * people Israel.*

The claim of the grieving heart in need of consolation is balanced with the claim of the wise mind that accepts death.

Death is not an evil. It is a natural event which occurs to every living being. Death is not the opposite of life. Rather, life and death are interrelated parts of a continuum of existence, an eternal rhythm. A philosophy of death and a philosophy of life are not separable. Jewish tradition, in its balance of death defiance and death acceptance, puts both life and death in perspective.

11

THE NATION OF
ISRAEL

Why should so many people over so many centuries have desired to destroy the Jews? Why should anyone have cared about a small number of people who observed their own religion quietly and peacefully? Why, even today, do the nations of the world devote so much time and energy to criticizing, attacking, and calling for the extermination of the Jewish State, which has a total Jewish population of eight million out of the world population of over seven billion? Why do the nations of the world begrudge the Jewish people one tiny bit of land known as Israel, when the land of Israel occupies an infinitesimal amount of the territory of the earth? It makes no sense at all. And yet it is so. Apparently, the very existence of the Jewish people and of Israel represents a serious challenge to other peoples. They recognize that Israel's existence is indeed a miracle, but they do not want to admit this obvious fact. The very existence of the Jewish people is a thorn in the side of religions that claim to have superseded the religion of Israel, and to nations that reject the religious foundation that Israel has provided for much of our civilization.

The historian Fernand Braudel has noted that in spite of the ability of the Jewish people to adapt to many societies and situations over the centuries, they have maintained their "basic personality." The Jewish people have threaded their way through history and, against enormous odds, have not lost themselves in the process. The destiny of Israel, its strength, its survival, and its misfortunes are all the consequence of its remaining irreducible, refusing to be diluted—that is, of being "a civilization faithful to itself."[1]

The Torah and religious traditions of Israel have served to keep the Jews united in spirit, even when divided into communities throughout the world. Halakhah, Jewish law, has been a powerful influence for maintaining similarities in Jewish observances and practices wherever Jews have lived. The Jewish people, even in exile, always viewed themselves as part of the nation of Israel. The Torah and religious traditions were major components of the Jewish nation. Though living in exile for many centuries, the Jews never lost sight of the fact that they intended to return to their homeland in Israel. Their prayer books were filled with dreams of return. Wherever they lived, they viewed themselves as part of a Jewish nation in exile. They governed themselves according to their own laws. Although they conformed to the laws and customs of the societies in which they lived, the Jews remained tenaciously faithful to their own way of life. Jewish communities have always had their own rabbinic courts, religious schools, and communal institutions. The Jews formed themselves into *kehillot*, communities, and to the extent possible, they governed themselves. This was true of all Jewish communities until modern times.

Western civilization offered a serious challenge to Jewish nationhood by offering emancipation. Being allowed to leave their ghettos and to attend Western schools, to become citizens of the countries in which they lived, to participate fully in the cultural, spiritual, and economic life of their societies—many Jews were lured to the opportunities offered by the new openings. Emancipation brought many advantages to individual Jews but posed serious threats to Jewish nationhood. Jews in Germany and elsewhere in Europe assimilated so quickly that many defected from Jewishness altogether by converting to the dominant faith. Jewish religious observances struck "enlightened" Jews as being archaic. A literature sprouted up among the Jews that reflected the tremendous turmoil within the community. On one side were the reformers; and on the other were the traditionalists who feared making unnecessary accommodations to the non-Jewish world. The first group preferred to assimilate, while the latter group preferred to remain in ghettos.

This intellectual struggle has characterized Jewish life from the late eighteenth century to our own time. The emergence of a political Zionist movement in the nineteenth century and the establishment of the State of Israel in 1948 have helped strengthen the Jewish notion of its own nationalism; but interestingly, the conflict of the enlightenment continues to trouble Jews even now. There are still those who prefer to think of Judaism as distinct from Jewish nationalism. This dichotomy is essentially a reaction to emancipation and is not the classic, normative Jewish position.

Rabbi Eliyahu Benamozegh, an important nineteenth-century Italian intellectual figure, in his book *In Ethical Paths*, offers a comparison between Christian ethics and Jewish ethics. He notes that the Jewish tradition encompasses two different aspects: the national and the ethical. Jewish nationalism and Jewish ethics are intertwined and therefore, at first glance, seem to be less elevated than Christian ethics. But in reality, Christian ethics are not applicable to national life. They speak of humility, suffering, compassion, etc. Yet which nation on earth will allow itself to be attacked and not defend itself? Which will forgive debts or insults or cruelties against its people? In contrast, Jewish tradition is realistic in linking ethical teachings with national and practical concerns. The Torah is not merely a document that outlines the religion of Israel, but is also the national covenant between Israel and God.[2]

Rabbi Benzion Uziel's Vision of Nationhood

Rabbi Benzion Uziel devoted much thought to explaining Jewishness both in its religious and national dimensions. For example, he offered an interpretation of the traditional three weeks of mourning that are observed by Jewish people between the Hebrew dates of Tammuz 17 and Av 9. Both of those dates are fast days in commemoration of the siege and destruction of Jerusalem in ancient times. Rabbi Uziel suggests that the purpose of these weeks of national mourning is to seek the underlying reasons for the destruction of our national structure in antiquity:

Jewish mourning is not merely mourning over something lost which never returns; such mourning is an empty and vain task. What good is mourning for something which is lost and which will never return? Rather, our mourning on these days aims at clarifying the significance of our loss, and the lack within us created by our national destruction; and to search for ways to restore that which has been lost, to build that which has been destroyed, and to restore the ruins. And so our rabbis taught: all who mourn Jerusalem will merit to see its rejoicing.[3]

According to Rabbi Uziel, the national structure depends on three things: First, there must be a recognition of a national charter and a belief in the ability to achieve its goals. Second, there must be unified action toward fulfilling this charter. Third, there must be a homeland and independent state that is the place in which the national charter can be fulfilled. The first responsibility of a nation is to know itself: "An awareness of the charter in its clarity, and a belief in achieving it—these form the essential foundation upon which the entire national structure rests and sustains itself forever." It is vital, therefore, for Jews to be deeply aware of their own national character. "An uncertain faith or an erroneous faith is a fire which eats the foundations and a worm which gnaws at its soul." Those who lack faith and commitment live without purpose. They do not work for the sake of the goal but only for their own pleasure, to gain honor or money.

Rabbi Uziel states that Israel in its relation to the nations is like a prophet in relationship to the people. A prophet is one who received a message from God. One may not want to be a prophet but—once called by God—one has no option. Once the prophet understands clearly the meaning of the message, there is no choice but to deliver it. Likewise, Israel must understand its own divine message and must live according to it. This is the precise strength and greatness of Israel. When the Jews doubt or do not understand their own specific mission, they stumble and fall.

A nation does not exist on ideas alone, but needs specific actions. Spiritual uplift is not enough. Studying, praying, and thinking must

be supplemented by deeds. National ideals are empty unless they
are attached to behavior, unless they influence the way people live.
"The good deeds to which the spirit of a nation gives birth—these
are the mirror through which one can see the soul of the nation." During
the last period of the Second Temple, under the Romans, Jewish beliefs
were strong, but their religious actions were weakened. "Although we
did not follow the gods of Rome, yet the ways of Rome and its people,
its laws and statutes, entered into our land; and in this way our unity was
destroyed and our strength was sapped." Not living by our distinctive
way of life leads to our own destruction. Following the ways of others
reduces us. Without our even realizing what is happening to us, assimilation into other cultures robs us of our own identity.

Rabbi Uziel draws a lesson from the Sabbath.[4] The commandments
for the Sabbath are *zakhor*, remember, and *shamor*, observe. The two
go together like a flame and an ember. It is not enough to think of the
philosophy and to remember the meaning of the Sabbath, but one also
must perform specific activities in observance of the Sabbath. It is necessary to tie the ideals to a real world of action. He believes that those
who violate the laws of Shabbat thereby undermine a basic element of
Jewish nationhood. "Individual freedom is limited by national foundations and principles." Since the Sabbath is intrinsic to the nationhood of Israel, any Jew who violates it is threatening the well-being of
the entire people. The importance of a Jewish community, and of the
Jewish State, is to provide the social and political context for the real-
ization of Jewish religious ideals. A Jewish community or Jewish State
that abandons its own spiritual heritage in order to follow the ways of
other peoples is selling itself out.

Rabbi Uziel speaks of two kinds of gatherings.[5] One is a gathering in
a specific place where people come together for a united purpose. The
second is a spiritual gathering, a uniting around an encompassing idea
or thought. The individual communities of Jews in all the lands of the
dispersion and even in Israel are known as holy congregations (*kahal
kadosh*). Each *kahal* exists individually, but all stem from and are nur-
tured by the ideas that gather them together into one greater *kahal*— the
Jewish people. The ideas and values of the Torah serve as the unifying

and unique agents for the people of Israel. The political leader of Israel must have the power not only to gather the people to one place or to one political goal, but must also be able to relate to the spiritual life of Israel, to unite the people in their commitment to the Torah.

In explaining the mystery of Jewish survival, Rabbi Uziel has argued,

> In every place where Israel was exiled, they carried with them first and foremost their scrolls of the Torah. They built holy arks for them and made sanctuaries for prayer and gathering. They established yeshivot and schools to study Torah. Over all, they established a kingdom deep within themselves, in the form of rabbis and leaders of congregations.[6]

The unique national feature of Israel has been this sense of transcendent unity, a commitment to the spiritual ideas of the Torah, the commitment to Jewish values and observances even when these entailed great personal sacrifice.

Rabbi Uziel has taught, therefore, that the Torah provides meaning to Jewish peoplehood. Jews who do not understand or do not observe the teachings of the Torah contribute to a weakening of the entire Jewish people. Just as a prophet needed to understand God's message to be able to communicate it to others, so the people of Israel must understand its own charter—the Torah—before it can properly express its identity to others. Jewish peoplehood is based on divine revelation. That revelation created not just a religion but a nation.

Conversion to the Jewish People

The Jewish people has a national and religious identity. The idea of "faith" does not define Judaism as it does other religions. Even a Jew who does not have "faith" remains a Jew, part of the Jewish nation. But the Jewish nation is founded on a divine revelation. The religious and national character of the Jews are inextricably intertwined.

Perhaps the best way to understand what is entailed by the religion/ nationhood of Israel is to consider the question of conversion. How can a non-Jew join the people of Israel? What exactly must he accept? What does the proselyte convert to: a religion or a nation or both?

Gerut, conversion to the Jewish people, has become one of the most controversial issues confronting modern Jews.[7] The Jewish people has always welcomed sincere converts who wish to become part of the nation and religion of Israel and who willingly accept the responsibility of observing the commandments. However, in our times, many (perhaps most) candidates for conversion are not motivated by an objective love and commitment to Judaism or to the Jewish people. Rather, they are non-Jews who wish to marry Jewish partners, or who are already married to Jews and now wish to convert for the sake of their children. Often enough the candidates for conversion are not seriously interested in accepting the observance of all mitzvot and may even indicate so. Sometimes it is clear to the rabbis involved that the would-be convert will not in the immediate future be an observant Jew.

Rabbinic opinion has varied widely concerning conversions that have been motivated by sociological rather than theological considerations. Rabbi Abraham Isaac Kook insisted that only converts who agreed to be fully observant of Jewish commandments should be accepted. If a convert does not observe Jewish religious laws, then the conversion is not really proper. Moreover, those rabbis who accepted such a convert are blameworthy. In one case, Rabbi Kook ruled that a non-Jewish woman who converted for the sake of marriage and clearly had no religious dedication to the traditions of the Torah remained a non-Jew. The conversion ritual was meaningless. "And happy is the one who stands at the breach to guard the purity of Israel, may a blessing of good come to him."[8]

On the other hand, Rabbi Benzion Uziel argued that not only may we accept such converts, but it is actually a positive commandment to do so if we believe the conversion will help create a Jewish home. Even if we surmise that the convert will not be fully observant of our religious traditions, we should perform the conversion in order to prevent intermarriage or loss of children from the Jewish fold.[9]

Between these two positions, there is a wide variety of intermediate opinion. Since this issue is concerned with the very definition of Jewishness, it has evoked deep emotional reactions. This is not a debate on an abstract point of Jewish law: it touches the source of Jewish existence.

In contemporary Jewish life, the term *giyyur kahalakhah,* a conversion according to Jewish law, has become something of a battle cry. Among Orthodox Jews, any conversion that is not done in accordance with traditional Jewish law is an attack on the integrity of the Jewish people. Conversions performed by non-Orthodox rabbis are generally regarded as being invalid. On the other hand, non-Orthodox spokesmen claim that the Orthodox should have no monopoly in determining who is really Jewish, who is an acceptable convert.

Debates on this topic have frightening implications. What is needed now is a fresh look at the primary sources dealing with conversion. We must begin at the beginning, with a definition of what makes a person Jewish.

Going back to the Bible, we find no specific mention of a formal procedure for conversion. Various non-Israelites had attached themselves to the people of Israel, e.g., the mixed multitude who joined the exodus from Egypt. Many laws are stated in the Torah on behalf of the *ger,* the non-Israelite stranger who lived among the Israelites in the land of Israel; but the biblical term *ger* does not seem to mean a full-fledged convert in the modern sense. In 2 Kings 17:32–3 and in Esther 8:17 we find references to groups who in some way attached themselves to the people of Israel. But there is no clear statement describing a conversion procedure.

The classic biblical example of a righteous convert is Ruth. She tells her Jewish mother-in-law: "Wherever you go, I shall go; and where you lodge, I shall lodge. Your people will be my people and your God will be my God." Ruth has served as a prototype of the ideal convert, one who accepts the Jewish people and religion sincerely and completely. Yet the details of the conversion process of Ruth are omitted from the text.

Yehezkel Kaufmann has described biblical conversion as *giyyur ha-artsi ha-tarbuti,* a non-Israelite's acculturation into the dominant Israelite culture.[10] Non-Israelites living in the Israelite land would naturally become absorbed by the national culture, accepting various social and religious mores in the course of time. Essentially, this was an ethnic conversion in which religion played a part. Kaufmann's observation seems fair. Even going back to the case of Ruth, we note that she first identified with the Israelite people and then with the Israelite God.

Who was an Israelite in biblical times? Anyone who was born into an Israelite family or anyone who assimilated into the people of Israel and became naturalized. The main factor was the nation or people of Israel. The strictly religious dimension of conversion did not yet exist.

Kaufmann asserts that after the Israelites were expelled from their land and lost their national center, a new type of *gerut* came into being—*giyyur ha-berit*, a conversion based exclusively on religion. A non-Jew now had to convert to Judaism, not to the culture and people of Israel. In biblical times, the stranger in the land of Israel gradually adopted Israelite patterns of life; in post-exilic times, the stranger could retain her own language and live in her own land and still convert to Judaism. Religion replaced land and nationality as the definition of an Israelite.

Yet if we consider the Talmudic sources dealing with conversion, we shall find that Kaufmann errs. The religion of Israel never replaced the people of Israel as the main element of self-definition. Even in Talmudic times, conversion was seen primarily as an act of joining the Jewish people, becoming part of the Jewish national destiny. A procedure was delineated for the conversion process, the religious dimension was stressed; but, in the final analysis, peoplehood was the main issue. There are two major Talmudic sources on this subject that bear examination.

1. Yavamot 47a–b:

> Our rabbis taught: if at the present time a person desires to become a proselyte, he is to be addressed as follows: "Why do you come to become a proselyte? Do you know that Israel at the present time is persecuted and oppressed, despised, harassed, and overcome by afflictions?" If he replies, "I know and yet am unworthy, he is

accepted forthwith and is given instruction in some of the minor and some of the major commandments ... and is also told of the punishment for transgression of the commandments. And as he is informed of the punishment for the transgression of the commandments, so is he informed of the reward granted for their fulfillment.... He is not, however, to be persuaded or dissuaded too much. [In the case of a man,] if he accepted, he is circumcised forthwith. As soon as he is healed, arrangements are made for his immediate ablution.....When he comes up after his ablution he is deemed to be an Israelite in all respects. In the case of a woman proselyte, women make her sit in the water up to her neck, while two [or three] learned men stand outside and give her instruction in some of the minor commandments and some of the major ones.

This passage is noteworthy for several reasons. First, we see that our initial comments to a would-be convert relate to the difficulties of being a member of the Jewish people. We must ascertain the willingness to share the burdens of our people, to share sincerely in our destiny. Only after we are satisfied on this score do we instruct "in some of the minor and some of the major commandments." Even when we do give this instruction, it is far from comprehensive, i.e., it does not include all the mitzvot, only some of them.

Moreover, we are not supposed to persuade or dissuade too much, but rather point out the pluses and minuses so that the candidate can make an informed decision. Upon the person's acceptance of the responsibilities, the conversion procedure is followed and the person is accepted as a complete Israelite.

Rabbi Benzion Uziel, considering this source, concludes that we do not ask the candidate to promise to fulfill the mitzvot, and it is not even necessary for the beit din to know that the mitzvot will be observed. The reason for informing the candidate of some of the commandments is simply to provide the opportunity to withdraw before it is too late.

This source indicates, then, that we are concerned about the convert's becoming a member of our people. One might argue that if a non-

Jew agreed to observe all our religious commandments but refused to identify as a member of our people, we would reject such a conversion. Indeed, Rabbi Shlomo Goren, late Ashkenazic chief rabbi of Israel, has so ruled. Accepting Judaism is not identical with becoming Jewish.[11]

We can analyze this point from a different perspective. A person born of a Jewish mother is halakhically regarded as a Jew. This person may be completely non-observant of our commandments, or an atheist; yet Jewish law always regards her as Jewish. If we think of being Jewish solely in terms of adhering to Judaism, this law is absurd. Obviously something else is involved, namely peoplehood. A person born of a Jewish mother is biologically part of our people, regardless of personal feelings or behavior. By being born Jewish, one is linked to Jewish destiny and may never be written off completely. (Just as a parent who disowns a child, or vice versa, does not sever the biological relationship. The relationship is fixed and eternal.) Being Jewish means being part of the Jewish people. Judaism is the religion of our people but it is not the definition of our Jewishness.

2. Yavamot 24*b*

"If a man is suspected of [intercourse] ... with a heathen who subsequently became a proselyte, he must not marry her. If, however, he did marry her, they need not be separated."

Gemara: This implies that she may become a proper proselyte. But against this a contradiction is raised. Both a man who became a proselyte for the sake of a woman and a woman who became a proselyte for the sake of a man ... are not proper proselytes. These are the words of R. Nehemiah, for R. Nehemiah used to say: Neither lion proselytes nor dream proselytes nor the proselytes of Mordecai and Esther are proper proselytes unless they become converted as at the present time.... Surely concerning this it was stated that R. Isaac b. Samuel b. Martha said in the name of Rab: the halakhah is in accordance with the opinion of him who maintained that they are all proper proselytes. The Talmud is here concerned with people who convert for ulterior motives—marriage, fear, dreams, etc. Rabbi Nehemiah argues that such conversions are not valid. But his opinion is rejected. The conclusion—and the accepted law—is that such conversions are indeed valid.

What is the basis for this discussion? Rabbi Nehemiah thinks that individuals who do not convert for idealistic, theological, and philosophical reasons are to be rejected. This opinion makes good sense if we view the conversion process as one in which the non-Jew's primary decision is to accept Judaism. If she wants to be Jewish for practical considerations but does not genuinely have a belief in and commitment to Judaism, then the conversion process is a sham, an empty ceremonial.

But Rabbi Nehemiah's opinion is rejected. One who converts even with ulterior motives is a valid convert. The law can be understood only if we assume that conversion means becoming part of the Jewish people. If a non-Jew chooses to join our ranks he may do so even if not accepting Judaism from theological convictions. A non-Jew who wants to marry someone Jewish and to raise Jewish children has opted to become part of our people, even though the commitment to our religion may be less than perfect.

Another Talmudic passage points in the same direction. Rab and Samuel speak of a proselyte who became converted among the Gentiles and did not even know the fundamental laws of the Sabbath (*Shabbat* 68a). Rabbi Moshe Feinstein noted that such a convert is valid even if still far removed from observing the mitzvot.[12] This proselyte identified with the Jewish people although his knowledge of Judaism was quite deficient.

In fact, there is no Talmudic legal source that would indicate unequivocally that acceptance of all commandments is a prerequisite for conversion. The central concern of Talmudic as well as biblical times is the proselyte's commitment to the Jewish people.

What does it mean to become part of the Jewish people? How can we measure the commitment of a would-be convert to our people? Obviously more than a token or casual commitment to our people is required. To think otherwise is to degrade our people and our history. It is not possible to codify exact guidelines as to what does or does not constitute a genuine commitment to the people of Israel. The final decision in this matter is really left to the rabbis who are involved in each case. Each candidate for conversion has her own dynamics and must be evaluated individually.

Some cases, though, seem clearly to be acceptable. A non-Jewish spouse of a Russian Jew who sacrificed much to emigrate to Israel and to join our people is one example. A non-Jewish partner in marriage who wishes to convert in order to raise the children with a Jewish identity is another. Where it can be determined that the non-Jew is sincerely dedicated to sharing our destiny, carrying our burdens, participating in our communal life, there is a good basis for conversion. Certainly we must make every effort to inform candidates for conversion of the beliefs and principles of Judaism, of our mitzvot and customs. These are basic factors in the life of our people.

In returning to our classic biblical and Talmudic sources, we have arrived at an old but novel understanding of Jewishness. By stressing this view, we can hope to deal more successfully with the contemporary disputes about *gerut*. Certainly much rabbinic literature has been created since Talmudic times, and the earlier concept of conversion has been blurred in the process. It is all the more important, then, to go back to our primary sources and look at them objectively. The Talmudic halakhic sources are far more open to receiving proselytes to the Jewish people than some who argue strenuously in the name of halakhah may want to admit. There is certainly ample support to perform conversions for the sake of marriage if the convert has a commitment to identify as a Jew, raise children as Jews, settle in Israel, etc.

Israel and the Nations

Israel has always viewed itself as a nation chosen by God: Israel and God entered a covenant, with the Torah being the document describing this covenant. Interestingly, the Torah does not speak of Israel bringing its message to the other peoples of the world. Even the later prophetic idea that Israel should be the "light unto the nations" does not mean that the people of Israel were obligated to convert all the people of the world to the Israelite nation/religion.

The Torah is a document describing the relationship between God and Israel. The Israelites are bound to the terms set forth in the Torah, the oral law, and halakhah in general. Other peoples may have their own chosenness, may follow their own paths to God. Rabbinic tradition teaches that there are seven Noahide laws that all human beings must observe, and that form the basis of simple morality and justice in the world. But beyond these elementary laws of decency, Jewish tradition does not teach that non-Jews must become Jews. On the contrary, Jewish tradition holds that there is certainly a place in the world-to-come for all righteous people, whether Jewish or not.

Chosenness, therefore, has been viewed as a private matter between God and Israel. It is neither a sign of superiority nor inferiority—just a historical fact. Even in the end of days, it is not expected that the non-Jews of the world will all convert to become members of the Jewish people/religion. The prophetic belief that in messianic times everyone will recognize the true One God does not mean that everyone will become Jewish. It is possible to have a true notion of the One God, to be a righteous person, and yet not become part of the Jewish nation.

The Torah is directed to the people of Israel. God promised Abraham that his descendants would dwell in the Promised Land. Israelite history cannot be understood without reference to the central role that the land of Israel has played and does play in Jewish national/religious life. Since the Israelite nation is attached to the land of Israel, it is obviously bound by these limitations. All the lands of the earth cannot be Israel, and all the peoples of the world cannot be Israelites. There are many roads to God, with Israel following its own distinctive way. Those who wish to join Israel are welcomed. But it is not likely, and not expected, that a very high percentage of the world population will do so.

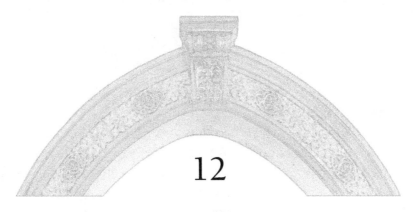

12

FAMILY, SOCIETY, INDIVIDUAL

In a thoughtful little volume, *Culture and Commitment*, Margaret Mead offered a study of the generation gap.[1] She described three different kinds of culture, each with its own strengths and weaknesses; and she tried to understand contemporary life based on her understanding of these cultures.

A postfigurative culture is one in which the past is the guide to the future. Such cultures are generally quite stable and tradition oriented. They are characterized by veneration of elders. Parents can predict with reasonable accuracy what their children's lives will be like. Children inherit beliefs, mannerisms, and ways of thinking from their elders. The postfigurative culture is so stable and tradition bound that there are few surprises within it. People are born, they live, and they die—all within a relatively predictable pattern.

In a cofigurative culture, the elders have lost their role as guides. Rather, the new generation learns from peers. An example of a cofigurative culture may be found among immigrants to a new land. To children being raised in a new environment, their parents and grandparents represent the old world, the world that they are trying to leave. Children learn from their native-born contemporaries. A gap opens between the generations. The more elders try to force the old ways on the young, the more the young will rebel.

Margaret Mead suggests that contemporary American society is a prefigurative culture. There has been a radical break with past patterns of culture. Presently, the elders and the youngers are all immigrants in a new world of technology, space exploration, etc. No one can say what life will be like in ten years or fifty years. It changes so fast and so universally that elders and youngers are all in the same predicament. While a gap remains between generations, this gap can be dealt with sympathetically once everyone realizes that a new reality exists. If the elders have lost their authority, so have the younger contemporaries. No one seems to have the correct answers for the future. And so there is social turmoil.

This analysis of culture, although much simplified, provides a thoughtful framework for considering the nature of human societies. The categories apply, in varying ways, to developments among the Jewish people over the centuries.

At base, the religious culture of the people of Israel has many post-figurative elements. The Torah commands respect for parents in particular, and for elders in general. The leaders of the people are known as elders. Tradition is venerated; and it is the elders who understand the traditions best, and who are obliged to transmit them to the new generations. The Torah emphasizes the responsibility of the elders to teach the youngers. The Haggadah of Passover captures the essential Jewish spirit. It is an elaborate format for the elders to recount the miracles of God when He redeemed the Israelites from slavery in Egypt. The Haggadah describes the responsibility of transmitting the story to children, whether they are wise, wicked, simple, or even if they do not know how to ask. The point is, the elders are obligated to transmit the story; just as the youngers are obligated to learn it.

Historically, laws of honoring parents and teachers have made it clear to the young generation that it is the elders who have the authority. The codes of Jewish law have included such regulations as the requirement for children to stand when their parents enter the room, not to sit in their parents' chairs, not to contradict their parents, not even to agree with their parents in public since the opinions of parents do not need the approval of children.

Many customs have arisen throughout the Jewish world that emphasize respect for parents, teachers, and elders. For example, among

Sephardic Jews, whenever an older relative or a teacher is called to read from the Torah scroll, all younger relatives and students stand in respect. It has also been customary for children to kiss the hands of their parents and grandparents in order to receive their blessings. Among many Sephardim, children are named after living grandparents. The first-born son is named after the father's father, the second-born son after the mother's father; the first-born daughter after the father's mother; and the second-born daughter after the mother's mother. The result of this custom has been to have a number of grandchildren carrying the same name as their grandparents. This practice tended to strengthen family ties, as well as inculcating in the youngsters the fact that they are named after grandparents and are expected to live according to the standards of their elders.

The Jewish people existed within a general postfigurative cultural pattern until the eighteenth century. And even then, many communities, especially those not in the West, continued their postfigurative cultural patterns well into the nineteenth and even twentieth centuries.

A cofigurative culture emerged among the Jews when a feeling developed that their elders no longer represented the "truth." With emancipation, Jews in Western Europe were anxious to become like the non-Jews around them. Many left their ghettos, physically and spiritually. To many, the old ways were viewed as archaic. The new opportunities of Western society were seen as great blessings. But, as often happens in cofigurative cultures, people soon realized that the substitute culture was shallow and had problems of its own. In cofigurative society, the feeling of connection with a solid past begins to erode. People may earn more money, have more advanced educational degrees, and live in nicer homes; but they are not necessarily happier than their grandparents or great-grandparents who lived in a postfigurative society. In fact, people in a cofigurative culture may very well be less happy than their less sophisticated ancestors.

Just as Margaret Mead has argued that moderns are now living in a prefigurative culture, the same holds doubly true for the Jewish people. This is clearly a new era for Jews. Emil Fackenheim, in his book *To Mend the World*, has argued that there has been a rupture in Jewish history.[2] The way we face life now is radically different from the way Jews faced life before the Holocaust. We can no longer speak of God with the same meaning as Jews who spoke of God before that disaster. While I disagree with Fackenheim's making the Holocaust the central event that ruptured the present from the past for the Jews, I agree that a rupture has indeed occurred. The Holocaust has been one aspect of the rupture. But it was the emergence of the State of Israel that has put the Jewish people into a prefigurative situation. We now have a generation of Jews who cannot remember living in a world without a Jewish State. When young Jews speak of Israel, of Jewish pride, of nationalism—they speak in terms that their elders do not understand in the same way. Things really are not the same. The ghetto Jew, the victim Jew are not acceptable for the young generation, though these patterns were acceptable to the older generations.

The old ideas of the postfigurative culture are inadequate for dealing with Jewish life and thought today. Elders telling the youngers the meaning of Jewishness, as though the elders still had their postfigurative authority, is a sad charade. Elders who speak of caution and who fear change represent impossible categories for many members of the younger generation to accept.

There has been a gap between Jewish thought and reality. Traditions are maintained, even when they no longer correspond to the current situation. For example, the wedding ceremony includes a prayer that God should restore the sound of brides and grooms in the streets of Jerusalem. Yet the sound of brides and grooms *can* be heard among Jews in Jerusalem today! The ritual has not yet adjusted to the new reality. Rabbi Haim David Halevy has written that it is inappropriate for Jews to recite the traditional prayer on the ninth of Av that asks God to console Jerusalem, "the city which is destroyed, humiliated, empty, without its children."[3] Rabbi Halevy points out that it is not proper to say these words, since they are no longer true. He has emended the text to read that God should have mercy on Jerusalem, which *was* destroyed, humiliated, empty, without her children. For this very small and very reasonable emendation, Rabbi Halevy was criticized sharply by many traditionalists. These are just small examples demonstrating that not everyone has yet been able to grasp the new situation in which Jews find themselves today.

This is a new era in Jewish life. The old patience and the old axioms are not totally satisfactory. Most Jews no longer live in a stable, postfigurative cultural setting. The more one insists on pretending that everything is the same as it always was, that everything is just a natural progression and development, the more one is removed from reality.

The old generations and the young generations of Jews are in a prefigurative culture. We are all immigrants in a new world, a world where Israel is a nation, where Jews assert their national and religious identity without fear or apology. While the past provides guidelines, it does not provide all the answers. The elders need to understand the impatience and confidence of the young. The young need to understand the traditionalism and patience offered by the old. And we all need to understand clearly that the future is uncertain, that we need to work together as immigrants in a new era of the Jewish adventure.

The last several centuries have been turbulent for the Jewish people. Westernization and assimilation have challenged the fabric of Jewish life. The Holocaust wiped out six million Jews—one-third of the entire Jewish population of the time—in just a few years. The State of Israel has been involved in one war after another just to ensure its survival. The physical and spiritual fragmentation within the Jewish community is staggering. The word "Jew" encompasses individuals of vastly different religious, political, social, and economic outlooks. Elias Canetti, in his book *Crowds and Power*, has observed about the Jews:

> Fools may tell stories of their sameness everywhere, but anyone who knows them well will be inclined to think that there are more varied types among them than among any other people. The extent of variation between Jews, both in their nature and their appearance, is one of the most extraordinary phenomena there is.[4]

Jews, then, are part of a prefigurative culture in two senses. First, like all other human beings in the modern world, Jews recognize the unpredictability of the future due to advances in technology. Second, the Jews are in the midst of their own specific prefigurative culture, a new Jewish era, where the future also is unpredictable and uncertain, where there has been a rupture with the past.

Since the latter nineteenth century, millions of Jews have left their towns and villages in Russia, Poland, and throughout Eastern Europe. Many of the historic Jewish communities of the Muslim world have all but disappeared, with hundreds of thousands of Jews moving to Israel, the United States, and other parts of the world. Demographically and psychologically, the Jewish people today are in a very different place than they were in the premodern era. And yet the Torah was given for all generations. It offers guidance and a social structure that can meet the needs of Jews, even when the postfigurative model has been irrevocably altered.

Understanding the Context of Life

In Western society we are raised to respect and value individualism. Our society stresses individual achievement. We are fascinated by stories of people who were raised in poverty but who became fantastically wealthy due to their own hard work, ambition, and talent. As a culture we idolize "stars," individuals who stand out above all others for their excellence in a particular field. Our society is competitive. Each child learns at an early age that he must outdo others in order to succeed. He is encouraged to make a name for himself, to be distinguished from the crowd. Our American cultural heroes are rugged individualists who show courage and take risks. Individual rights and individual freedoms are highly prized features of our society.

Although Jewish tradition respects the individual, its main focus is on family, community, and nation. Even individual achievements have been evaluated not by how much the individual has done for herself, but by how much she has done for family and community. Instead of being a self-centered, individualistic culture, Jewish tradition has stressed the importance of collectivity. This point becomes very clear when we look at the ceremonies connected with the cycle of life.

When a baby boy is born, he is circumcised on the eighth day in order to enter the covenant of Abraham our father. Before the boy has any awareness of his own separate identity, he is made part of a covenant, part of the destiny of the people of Israel. Those present at a circumcision bless the child's parents with the following words:

> *May it be God's will that as you have been privileged*
> *to introduce your son into the covenant,*
> *so may you also be privileged to bring him to the Torah,*
> *the commandments, to the marriage canopy, to a life of good deeds;*
> *and let us say amen.*

Significantly, the blessing is not aimed at the child's health, wealth, or ability to make great achievements. Rather, the goal for that child is to learn the Torah, to observe the commandments, to get married, and to continue the cycle of the Jewish people. Following the naming ceremony, a blessing is given to the child asking God to help him attain the life of Torah, commandments, marriage, and good deeds. The expectations of the family, community, and people are clearly enunciated.

In the traditional Sephardic naming ceremony for baby girls, the text does wish the baby health, peace, and contentment. It goes on to pray that her parents have the merit of seeing her happily married, a radiant mother of children, rich in honor and joy to a ripe old age. The expectation for the girl, then, is to grow up in good health and strength so that she can marry and have children. Again, the overriding concern is for the continuity of the family and of the people. The individual is important as a building block in the structure of the generations.

The wedding ceremony provides further insight into the Jewish attitude on life. When a man betroths a woman, a blessing is recited praising God who has sanctified Israel with His commandments, who has provided laws of marriage. It concludes:

> *Blessed are You, Lord,*
> *who sanctifies Your people Israel by the rite of the wedding canopy*
> *and the consecration of betrothal.*

It is noteworthy that the blessing makes no particular reference to the man and woman who are entering a marriage relationship. It does not speak to their individual needs or aspirations. Rather, it provides the context of their life: a life of holiness, a life governed by God's commandments. At the time of betrothal, when a new link is about to be established in the generations of the Jewish people, we stop to reflect, and to bless God for having sanctified His people Israel. Marriage, and the continuity of generations that it implies, is part of God's plan for us.

The marriage ceremony has six blessings, following the blessing over wine. These blessings reflect the traditional Jewish philosophy of life.

> *Blessed are You, Lord our God, ruler of the universe,*
> *who has created all for Your glory.*

This blessing indicates the context of life. God is Master of the universe, and we are grateful to Him for our very existence.

> *Blessed are You, Lord our God, ruler of the universe,*
> *creator of adam (humanity).*

God decided to populate the earth by creating Adam: one individual. A mishnah in tractate *Sanhedrin* (4:5) comments that God created only one person in order to emphasize the significance of each individual. If anyone murders one human being, it is as though a universe has been destroyed. Each human life has immense value. The marriage ceremony makes reference to this uniqueness of each human being, of each of the marriage partners.

> *Blessed are You, Lord our God, ruler of the universe,*
> *who has created man in Your image.*
> *In the likeness of that image You did ordain for him woman made*
> *from him for perpetual human succession.*
> *Blessed are You, Lord, creator of adam (humanity).*

This blessing refers to Adam and Eve, both created in the image of God. When God first created Adam, the Torah states that He created Adam as male and female. In a later account, the Torah states that God put Adam to sleep and created woman from one of Adam's bones. This wedding blessing refers to God's creation of man and woman and their ability to perpetuate the species together. Both male and female are vital to the world.

> *May Zion, that has been barren, rejoice and exult*
> *at the speedy, joyful ingathering of her children.*
> *Blessed are You, Lord, who causes Zion to rejoice in her children.*

This blessing obviously was composed after the Jews had been exiled from their land. The desire to return to the national homeland was so strong that a blessing was incorporated into the wedding ceremony. Each Jewish couple was reminded of Zion and Jerusalem during their wedding. In fact, we mention the happiness of Zion before making any blessings referring to the happiness of bride and groom.

Thus far, the wedding blessings have followed a pattern, praising God for:

1. The creation of everything, i.e., giving meaning to existence
2. The creation and uniqueness of each individual
3. The special relationship of man and woman
4. The nation and land of Israel

Only after these blessings do we turn to the marriage couple directly. The last two blessings praise God as the One who gives joy to the bride and groom and who makes the bride and groom rejoice together. But even in the last blessing, when we refer specifically to the joy of the bride and groom, we also offer a prayer for the restoration of joy and happiness to the cities of Israel and the streets of Jerusalem.

The ceremonies described thus far provide a context for life. They emphasize that each individual is part of a greater reality—a people of

Israel, a holy nation. The individual is expected to find meaning in his life by sharing in the destiny of the people.

When we pray for someone who is ill, we ask that she may be healed together with other Israelites who are ill. When we console mourners, we pray that they may be consoled along with all the mourners of Zion and Jerusalem. The tendency to think of the needs of all Israel, rather than of individual needs, is characteristic of the Jewish prayer book in general. Almost all prayers are recited in the plural form. It is considered arrogance and bad manners for an individual to pray only on his own behalf.

Traditionally the family structure underscored the preeminence of the group rather than the individual. Children were named after grandparents or other relatives. They were part of a family tradition. Relatives often lived in the same neighborhood, so that each individual was actually part of a larger extended family. Since Jews were not allowed to travel on the Sabbath, they had to live within walking distance of their synagogue. In this way, Jewish neighborhoods became extensions of the family. The many festivals and observances of Jewish religion created a special feeling when experienced in a larger group. The neighborhood was an extension of home, a place filled with love, understanding, and extended family relationships. Individuals within a Jewish community were entitled to respect. Even in postfigurative Jewish families there was appreciation of individual talent, achievement, and dignity. Yet the individual was expected to use personal talents for the benefit of the family and community. Ideally Jews did not compete with each other, but worked with each other.

Clashes of Culture

Modern technological societies are individual oriented. Since so much of the world's scientific and technological progress has developed in the West, there is a pervasive assumption among Westerners that their culture is superior to others. Peoples of non-Western cultures are thought to be backward, or passive, or less gifted. After all, if they were as smart as we are, why didn't they make all these scientific achievements? Why are their societies still so underdeveloped in comparison to ours? Non-Western cultures may be viewed as being quaint, endowed with some ancient wisdom, as being superstitious, or primitive. But since Westerners are taught to compare and compete, they generally will conclude that the Western world is more advanced than, and therefore superior to, the non-Western world.

This attitude finds expression among Jews as well. Most Jews have been strongly influenced by Westernization. The majority of the world's Jewish population lives or originates in North America and Europe. A minority of the Jewish people have lived for centuries in North Africa and Asia. Western Jews have considered these non-Western Jews to be somewhat backward and uncivilized. During the late nineteenth and early twentieth centuries, Western European Jews established schools throughout Turkey, the Middle East, and North Africa in order to raise the standards of the hapless Jews in those backward countries. Indeed, economic, social, and educational conditions in those places were very bad by Western standards. The efforts of Western Jews to upgrade the condition of their non-Western coreligionists were noble and praiseworthy.

Yet few of the Westerners ever stopped to think that the non-Westerners had worthy cultural traits that deserved to be maintained. The cofigurative Jews of the West did not want to leave the postfigurative Jews of the East in tranquility. Western culture offered obvious advantages: advanced economic life, better standard of living, more systematic formal education. But in trying to "save" the non-Westerners, the unwritten agenda was to convert them into Westerners.

The Western–Eastern Jewish interrelationship became explosive with the establishment of the State of Israel. In 1948 the majority of Jews in Israel were of Western background. But shortly thereafter, hundreds of thousands of Jews from Africa and Asia poured into the new Jewish State. The immigrants were generally regarded as being backwards, unskilled, without leadership, without money, without technological expertise. The immigrants came from premodern, postfigurative cultures into a modern, technological, Western-oriented culture. The sparks of friction from the early meetings of these cultures were painful and agonizing for all the Jewish people. Even now, after several generations, the Western and non-Western Jewish cultures have not fully blended together. One of the reasons for the tension is that Westerners do not appreciate seriously the value of the culture of non-Westerners.

The real questions any culture must answer are: Do the people of this culture find meaning in life? Are they happy? Do their lives make sense to them? Obviously it is difficult to answer these questions with generalizations. Nevertheless it can be argued that the non-Western Jews historically were able to answer these questions with more confidence than Western Jews.

The characteristic features of the non-Western communities were postfigurative: emphasis on family, stability of the community, rootedness in tradition. People lived their lives with a deep religious sensitivity, understanding that life was created by God for His own glory. There was no need to compete against others, since the ultimate goal was to work for the betterment of all. Did life in this culture have meaning? Very much so. Were people happy? Yes, since they knew that their lives fitted into a family and community context. They were rooted. When they had problems, they had elders with whom they could discuss them. Was everything perfect in these societies? No, not at all. But individuals knew who they were, and what they were part of, and what they were expected to do with their lives.

In Western society, these questions cannot be answered so simply. It is not an accident that psychiatry and psychology were created in the West. People in the West are more likely to be deracinated, alienated, uncertain of the meaning of their lives. They enjoy the thrill of independence and individuality, but lack the stability that comes with a strong extended family, and an ancient venerated tradition. It is possible for a Westerner to have incredible wealth and all the technological devices and comforts—and yet to be miserable. Modern society tends to teach us constantly to strive, rather than to enjoy what we already have.

Living in a new prefigurative era, where many of the underpinnings of the past have been removed, creates a sense of uncertainty about the future. Thus it is all the more important that we recognize the wisdom of Jewish traditional values. It is wonderful to develop and utilize technology. But when all is said and done, conveniences and computers do not give life meaning. In all our striving, we seldom stop to pause to ask, Why are we doing this? What are the implications?

The new era of the Jewish people will find us utilizing Western efficiency, organization, and technology. But it will also find us placing more value on family, community, and tradition. We need individualistic courage; we also need traditional wisdom and calm.

Economic Life

The Torah describes a case where someone lends money to a poor person and takes a garment as pledge (Exodus 22:24–26). Since the poor person needs the garment in order to keep warm at night, the lender is commanded to return it to the borrower each evening. "For that is his only covering, it is his garment for his skin; wherein shall he sleep? And it shall come to pass, when he cries unto Me, that I will hear, for I am gracious." God becomes involved in this relatively simple economic relationship. From an abstract business point of view, one person lends money to another and takes a garment as a pledge. By right, the lender should hold the pledge until the borrower repays the debt. But the Torah teaches otherwise. The borrower and the lender are not engaged in a business relationship, but in a human relationship. The lender must return the pledge to the borrower even though this does not make good business sense. Perhaps the borrower will run away and not repay the debt. Nevertheless, the lender must give back the garment, and God Himself is on the side of the borrower.

This case exemplifies the Torah's attitude on economic life. Business is not conducted for its own sake, but for the benefit of all members of the community and society. The goal of economic life is to provide for everyone's needs as best as humanly possible. The Torah is not concerned with wealth for the sake of wealth. It is concerned with the well-being and dignity of the members of society.

The Torah legislation on behalf of the poor and oppressed is well-known. Farmers were obligated to leave portions of their fields unharvested, allocating it for the poor. Lenders were not allowed to charge interest on their loans to fellow Israelites. Society had an obligation to protect widows and orphans and all others who were vulnerable and unprotected. On each seventh year, debts were cancelled. On each fiftieth year, land was returned to the family who originally owned it. The result of these laws was to prevent chronic poverty within families. The younger generations did not inherit an overwhelming burden of debts from the older generations; and a family could look forward to a definite time when their property—which they may have had to sell in desperation—would be returned to them. Within Jewish tradition, charity is known as *tsedakah,* righteousness. Charity is not an option, but a commandment that one must fulfill. Even a poor person who lives off the contributions of others is obligated to share with others who are in need.

The highest form of *tsedakah* is providing employment, thereby allowing people to earn their own livings. Lending money at no interest is also especially praiseworthy, since this does not demean the poor person as would be the case if she were given alms. Economic life provides the framework for spiritual life.

Rabbi Benzion Uziel has analyzed the distinctive Jewish approach to economics. The Sabbath serves as an excellent example. For at least one-seventh of our lives we are free from physical labor and servitude. Shabbat teaches us that we are basically free. Some people object that resting from work on Shabbat hinders productivity. But they forget that human beings are supposed to be masters of the natural world, not slaves to it. "Man creates technology and reveals and exploits the powers of nature hidden in all sections of the creation; technology does not rule man and enslave him."[5] Shabbat does not only mean to rest, but to rest in holiness. It is the holiness of the day that sanctifies one's entire life.

Rabbi Uziel notes that the historic Jewish attitude calls on Jews to work. It is viewed as a commandment to work on the six days, just as it is a commandment to rest on the seventh. But the Jewish attitude on work differs from the attitude of those who see work as an end in itself, with the goal to increase production, increase wealth, increase technology. For Jewish tradition, labor is a means to an end, not an end in itself. Rabbi Uziel quotes the opinion of Rabbi Levi of the Talmud: "All of the actions of Israel differ from those of the nations of the world: in their plowing, planting, harvesting, winnowing, etc." The laws of the Torah govern all of these activities:

> There is no labor that lacks a specific set of [Torah] laws.... Labor itself is an intellectual and ethical sanctuary that elevates the soul, improves the spirit, and makes the workers into people of kindness, compassion, love, affection for all creations, open-hearted to all who are created in the image of God.[6]

Labor involves a relationship between owners and workers. It is based on honesty and trust. The Torah provides laws governing the responsibility and rights of employers and employees.

> Just as Torah without work will in the end be void, so also work which does not have with it Torah is not fit to be called by the name work.... The Torah of Israel is not hidden in the holy Ark in the synagogue, but goes with us in all our steps in all the places we go, enlightening us with its light and sanctifying us with its sanctity.... You cannot recognize the splendor of the Torah except as it appears in the thoughts and actions of a person and the nation of Israel, and you cannot recognize the form and structure of a Jew except in the Torah of God which is in the heart and the mitzvot of God which are in all one's deeds and actions.

Richard Rubenstein, in his book *The Age of Triage,* has drawn a candid picture of the way society has operated over the centuries.[7] As new methods of production developed, old forms of economic life were obliterated. Increased efficiency and technology have led to the need for less human labor. Rubenstein describes the process of triage, where natural forces or governments themselves eliminate unneeded, unproductive people. This was effected actively by encouraging emigration, or by actual destruction of populations. Triage was also accomplished passively, by eliminating the means of survival for segments of the population, so that they died of starvation or disease. Thomas Malthus suggested that poor people be moved to swampy, unhealthy areas so that they would catch diseases and die. In this way society would be rid of this unproductive group.

The process of triage is exacerbated by the incredible rush of technology in our own day. Many blue-collar workers suddenly find themselves redundant. The changes have come so quickly that many have been displaced without much prospect of finding other employment. Lives are ruined, families are broken—all in the name of economic progress.

The teachings of the Torah offer a sharp challenge to the prevailing economic policies of the industrialized nations. The Torah's first concern is with the well-being of people. Technology for its own sake is a monster. It is only important if it can improve the quality of people's lives. If it improves some lives and destroys others, it should be introduced gradually so that as few people as possible are hurt by the changes. And those who are displaced should never come to feel that they are redundant. They are also part of our society and need to be cared for and loved like anyone else. The value of a person's life is not measured by economic productivity.

Modern society relentlessly pursues a policy of rationalization of production. It constantly seeks technologies to produce things faster and more efficiently. We seldom stop to ask ourselves why we need to produce so much so quickly. Do people really need so much? And can people wait a little longer to get what they want?

We are in competition. Each company wants to produce more goods at a faster rate at lower cost per unit. This is called efficient productivity and makes a company competitive. Nations compete against each other, so even if we decide not to engage in the race, others would still be doing so. Then we would see ourselves as falling behind.

But what is the point of efficiency, productivity, cost per unit? Can the quality of our lives be measured simply by the gross national product figures? If our companies can produce more clothes than we can wear, more machinery than we can use, more cars than we can drive—why is this considered a sign of a successful economy? What happens to all the lives that have been uprooted in the technological rush?

Obviously, it is not likely that the process of rationalization of productivity will be stopped. Triage seems to be a fact of life in modern society. But perhaps the Torah's perspective on economic life can restore some idealism to modern business. The Torah teaches that the economy is created by humans to help humans. Our goal ought not to be how well we compete with others but how well we provide for all the needs of the people in our own society. Just as we work and produce things during the six days of the week, we need to rest in the holiness of Shabbat on the seventh day. And it is Shabbat that explains to us why we work on the six other days.

Modern society tends to focus on quantity. Jewish tradition focuses on quality. Modern society keeps asking: how much? Jewish tradition keeps asking: why?

Epilogue

A midrash tells that when the Almighty was about to create Adam, a debate broke out among the angels (*B'reishit Rabbah* 8:5). Some advised Him not to create human beings; others urged him to create humanity. *Hesed* (compassion) said: Let human beings be created because they will do acts of kindness. *Emet* (truth) said: Let them not be created because they will be filled with lies. *Tsedek* (righteousness) said: Create them because they will do acts of justice. *Shalom* (peace) said: Don't create them because they will be filled with strife.

God then cast *Emet* down to earth. The angels objected: Why did you treat *Emet* disrespectfully, since truth is Your hallmark? God replied: The truth will blossom forth from the earth.

And then Adam was created.

At the very point of the creation of humanity, this midrash teaches, it was clear that human beings would be a mixed blessing. They would form a society filled with lies and strife—but also filled with compassion and peace. In weighing the pluses and minuses, God opted for creating humanity. He planted truth into the soil of the earth with the confidence that one day truth will blossom and humanity will be redeemed.

In rabbinic tradition, Moses is identified with truth and Aaron is identified with compassion. God chose to give commandments through both of them. If Moses was often strong and demanding, Aaron was often resilient and kind. Moses and Aaron represent two essential qualities—truth and compassion—that together can tilt humanity in the right direction.

The Jewish people, over these past thousands of years, have sought to live according to the ideals and laws taught by Moses and Aaron. We have been impressively committed to finding a proper balance between truth and compassion; we have sought the redemption of humankind by seeking ultimate truth, and by rejecting the falsehoods and idolatries that fill the human imagination. We have stressed the centrality of lovingkindness and charity.

There has long been a dissonance between our inner world of truth and compassion and the external world in which we live, a world in which lies and violence abound. Throughout the ages Jews have been subjected to one persecution after another; every sort of lie has been lodged against us; we have been maligned and murdered generation after generation. We look around at our world today and see malignant anti-Semitism and anti-Zionism. We see anti-Jewish lies go unchallenged; we see terrorism against Jews idealized; we see a world full of "good people" who stand by and do nothing or say nothing in defense of the Jewish people.

And yet we persist in our inner spiritual world. We say our prayers each day. We maintain faith in God and in the ultimate redemption of humanity. Our faith in God is remarkable; but our faith in humanity is even more remarkable. After all we have experienced, can we really believe that people will change for the better, that their hatred and lies and violence will come to an end?

The figure of Moses reminds us that we cannot compromise in our search for truth. We cannot shy away from the demand for genuine justice. The figure of Aaron reminds us that we must not forget about human frailty and fear. We cannot lose sight of compassion and peace. Jewish life—and human life in general—must be a dynamic process of thinking and growing and courageous commitment to those values that redound to the glory of humanity. When we see ugly behavior and hear ugly words around us, we realize how far humanity still is from fulfilling God's hopes for us.

God cast *Emet* to the earth, indicating that the day will surely come when truth will blossom forth, when individuals and nations will admit their lies and injustices and cruelties. On that day, not only will the Jews be redeemed, but so will all the nations of the world. Truth will become so clear that all human beings will cleanse their souls and recognize the hand of God in history.

When we strive to internalize the teachings and characteristics of Moses and Aaron, we bring more truth and compassion into the world. In our day-to-day lives, these little steps may seem trivial in the face of the many problems confronting us and humanity. Yet in the cosmic struggle for the soul of humankind, we move the world a little closer to the day when truth will blossom forth from the earth. May this day come sooner rather than later.

Acknowledgments

This book emerged from a series of courses I gave for Congregation Shearith Israel and Sephardic House. An underlying concern of the classes was to deal with the basic patterns of Jewish living and to explore their meaning for modern Jews.

The first edition of this book was published by Sepher-Hermon Press and Sephardic House in 1986. Jason Aronson issued a soft-cover edition in 1997.

I am grateful to Stuart M. Matlins of Jewish Lights for making available this new, revised edition of the book. I thank Emily Wichland, Rachel Shields, Tim Holtz, and the rest of the staff at Jewish Lights for their efforts on behalf of this project.

A special word of thanks goes to my son, Rabbi Hayyim Angel, whose various suggestions have been incorporated into this new edition.

My wife, Gilda, was of inestimable assistance in all phases of the development of this book. Her many profound and sensitive insights are reflected throughout the work. I thank her and our children, Hayyim and Maxine Angel, Ronda Angel and Dr. Dan Arking, and Elana Angel and Dr. James Nussbaum; and our grandchildren, Jake Nussbaum, Andrew Arking, Jonathan Arking, Max Nussbaum, Charles Nussbaum, Jeremy Arking, Kara Nussbaum, Aviva Angel, Dahlia Angel, and Mordechai Pinhas Angel.

I thank the Almighty for having brought me to this special moment.

Notes

Chapter 1: The Rhythms of Nature

1. *Targum Yerushalmi*, Genesis 1:1. See also Benzion Uziel, *Hegyonei Uziel*, (Jerusalem, 5713 [1953]), 1:1.
2. *Mishneh Torah, Yesodei HaTorah* 2:2.
3. *B'reishit Rabbah* 1:1. There are a number of rabbinic sources expressing the belief that the Torah predated Creation. Among them are *B'reishit Rabbah* 1:4; *Vayikra Rabbah* 19:1; *Pesahim* 54a.
4. *Avodah Zarah* 3a.
5. See Solomon Schechter, Appendix A, *Studies in Judaism: Second Series* (Philadelphia: Jewish Publication Society, 1908), 297.
6. Mircea Eliade, *The Sacred and the Profane: The Nature of Religion* (New York: Harvest Books, 1959), 156.
7. Gershom Scholem, *On the Kabbalah and Its Symbolism* (New York: Schocken Books, 1965), 152–3.
8. See Schechter, Appendix A, p. 294.
9. David ben Joseph ben David Abudraham, *Abudraham haShalem* (Jerusalem: Usha Press, 5723 [1963]), 345–6. For laws and customs relating to the blessing of the moon see Haim David Halevy, *Mekor Hayyim* (Jerusalem, 5743 [1982]), 3:181–182; and Yaacob Huli, *Me'am Lo'ez* on Genesis 1:19.
10. Solomon Zeitlin, *The Rise and Fall of the Judean State: A Political, Social and Religious History of the Second Commonwealth*, 2nd ed. (Philadelphia: Jewish Publication Society, 1968), 1:248f.
11. See Halevy, *Mekor Hayyim*, 2:97.

Chapter 2: The Limitations of Systematic Theology

1. Alan Watts discusses the differences between Eastern and Western perceptions of reality in his many writings. In particular, see *The Book: On the Taboo Against Knowing Who You Are* (New York: Vintage Books, 1972); *Nature, Man and Woman* (New York: Vintage Books, 1970); *Psychotherapy*

East and West (New York: Vintage Books, 1961); *The Wisdom of Insecurity: A Message for an Age of Anxiety* (New York: Vintage Books, 1951).

2. For a discussion of Rabbi Luria's attitude on words, see Gershom Scholem, *Major Trends in Jewish Mysticism,* rev. ed. (New York: Schocken Books, 1967), 254.

3. Yosef Hayyim, *Mashal veNimshal* (Jerusalem, 1913), 35b.

Chapter 3: The Rhythms of Time

1. Eliade, *The Sacred and the Profane,* 70.
2. Ibid., 88.
3. Ibid., 107.
4. Ibid., 110.
5. There is a debate in the Talmud as to whether the universe was created in what we call Tishri or Nissan. The popularly accepted view is that God created the world on Rosh Hashanah, i.e., Tishri. See tractate *Rosh Hashanah* 11a.
6. Eliade, *The Sacred and the Profane,* 78.
7. Hans Meyerhoff, *Time in Literature*, quoted in Yosef Hayim Yerushalmi, *Zakhor: Jewish History and Jewish Memory* (Seattle: University of Washington Press, 1982), 79.
8. Elazar Azikri, *Sefer Hareidim* (Jerusalem, 1958), 47.

Chapter 4: Sacred Places

1. Becker, *The Denial of Death* (New York: Free Press, 1973), 26.
2. Ibid.
3. Eliade, *The Sacred and the Profane*, 25.
4. See Halevy, *Mekor Hayyim* 2:199.

Chapter 5: The Rhythms of Everyday Life

1. The prayers to be recited in connection with the rhythms of everyday life may be found in any Orthodox prayer book. The laws and customs relating to these rhythms are recorded in all of the codes of Jewish law. An especially good discussion is found in Halevy, *Mekor Hayyim*, vol. 1.
2. Becker, *The Denial of Death*, 33.

Chapter 6: Halakhah, the Jewish Way of Life

1. Maimonides discusses the definition of the oral law in the introduction to his commentary on the Mishnah. See *Guide of the Perplexed*, trans. Shlomo Pines (Chicago: University of Chicago Press, 1963).

2. Benzion Uziel, *Mikhmanei Uziel* (Tel Aviv, 1939), 358.
3. Ibid., 371.
4. Ibid., 376.
5. Ibid., 382.
6. Ibid., 391.
7. The material in this section is drawn from my article, "A Sephardic Approach to Halakhah," *Midstream* (August/September 1975), 66–69.
8. Rabbi Simhah ben Joshua of Zalozhtsy's travel account is found in J. D. Eisenstein, *Ozar haMasaot* (Tel Aviv, 1969), 241.
9. Alan Watts, *The Supreme Identity: An Essay on Oriental Metaphysics and the Christian Religion*, 2nd ed. (New York: Pantheon Books, 1972), 128.
10. André Chouraqui, *Between East and West: A History of the Jews of North Africa* (Philadelphia: Jewish Publication Society, 1968), 61.
11. H. J. Zimmels, *Ashkenazim and Sephardim* (London: Oxford University Press, 1969), 128f.
12. Uziel, *Mikhmanei Uziel,* 407.
13. The text of this contract is found in Yehoshua Benveniste, *Sha'ar Yehoshua* (Husiatyn, 1904), n. 2.
14. Tam ben Yahia, *Tumat Yesharim*, Venice, 1622, no. 213, 112b.
15. See "Safed in the Sixteenth Century—A City of Legists and Mystics," in *Studies in Judaism*, 208.
16. Isidore Epstein, *The Responsa of Rabbi Simon Duran as a Source of History of the Jews in North Africa* (New York: KTAV Publishing, 1968), 58–59.
17. David ibn Abi Zimra, *Responsa* (New York, 5727 [1966]), 1:308.
18. See Hayyim Yosef David Azulai's commentary on *Ethics of the Fathers* 103b.
19. Ibid., 97b.
20. Schechter, Appendix A, 292.
21. Chouraqui, *Between East and West*, 63. On the veneration of tombs of the righteous, see 71ff.

Chapter 7: Revelation

1. Uziel, *Mikhmanei Uziel*, 27f.
2. Ibid., 37f.
3. Moshe Cordovero, *Sefer Kavvanoth* (Tel Aviv, 1971), 59a. See also Scholem, *On the Kabbalah and Its Symbolism*, 65.
4. See Maimonides' discussion in his introduction to his commentary on the Mishnah in *Guide of the Perplexed*.
5. See Schechter, "Safed in the Sixteenth Century."

6. Vital's statements appear in his work *Sha'arei Kedushah*, 3:5–6, 8. See also R. J. Z. Werblowsky, *Joseph Karo, Lawyer and Mystic*, 2nd ed. (Philadelphia: Jewish Publication Society, 1977), 74f.

7. See the introduction to Yosef Karo, *Maggid Mesharim* (Jerusalem: Orah, 1960).

8. Werblowsky, *Joseph Karo, Lawyer and Mystic*, 286.

Chapter 8: Transcending the Self

1. Judah Abravanel, *The Philosophy of Love,* trans. F. Friedeberg-Seeley and Jean H. Barnes (London: Soncino Press, 1937), 55.

2. Ibid., 60.

3. For a discussion of techniques developed by Jewish mystics, see Aryeh Kaplan, *Meditation and Kabbalah* (York Beach, ME: Samuel Weiser, 1982); and *Jewish Meditation: A Practical Guide* (New York: Shocken Books, 1985).

4. Azikri, *Sefer Hareidim*, 214.

5. Ibid., 215.

6. Moshe Cordovero, *Sefer Gerushin* (Shklov, 5551 [1791]).

7. Ibid., 3a.

8. Moshe Cordovero, *The Palm Tree of Deborah*, trans. Louis Jacobs (London: Vallentine, Mitchell, 1960), 47.

9. Abravanel, *The Philosophy of Love*, 49.

10. *Sefer Kavvanoth* (Tel Aviv, 1971), 17a.

11. Abravanel, *The Philosophy of Love*, 201.

12. Hayyim Yosef David Azulai, *Avodat Hakodesh* (Warsaw: P. Lewensohn, 1879), 6.

13. See the treatise on humility (*Sha'ar Hak'niah*) in Bahya ibn Pakuda, *Duties of the Heart*, trans. Moses Hyamson (New York: Feldheim, 1978).

14. Moshe Hayyim Luzzatto, *Mesillat Yesharim*, section on acquiring humility.

15. Cordovero, *The Palm Tree of Deborah*, 47f.

Chapter 9: Providence

1. Maimonides, *Guide of the Perplexed*, chapter 51.

2. See the morning service for the Ninth of Av, *Seder Arba Ta'aniyoth* (Vienna: Josef Schlesinger's Buchhandlung, 1926), 182f.

3. *Mishneh Torah,* Laws of Repentance, 8:1–5. See also Maimonides' introduction to *Helek,* chapter 10 of *Sanhedrin* in *Guide of the Perplexed.*

4. Gershom Scholem, *The Messianic Idea in Judaism: And Other Essays on Jewish Spirituality* (New York: Schocken Books, 1972), 3.

5. Uziel, *Hegyonei Uziel*, 1:37.

6. Moshe Hayyim Luzzato, *Da'at Tevunot* [The Knowing Heart], trans. Shraga Silverstein (New York: Feldheim, 1982).

7. Harold S. Kushner, *When Bad Things Happen to Good People* (New York: Avron, 1983). See especially his discussion on pp. 37ff.

8. This idea is woven throughout his book. See Lewis Thomas, *The Lives of a Cell: Notes of a Biology Watcher* (New York: Penguin Books, 1975).

9. Ibid., 26.

10. See the commentary of Hayyim Ben Attar, *Or haHayyim*, on Genesis 1:17.

11. Yehudah Halevy, *The Kuzari: An Argument for the Faith of Israel*, trans. H. Hirschfeld (New York: Schocken Books, 1968), part 1, especially 44f.

Chapter 10: Confronting Death

(Much of the material in this chapter was first presented by me at the annual meeting of the Association of Orthodox Jewish Scientists, February 1984.)

1. Elias Canetti, *The Torch in My Ear* (New York: Farrar, Straus & Giroux, 1982), 50.

2. Becker, *The Denial of Death*, 53.

3. Philippe Aries, *The Hour of Our Death* (New York: Oxford University Press, 1981), 28. For a discussion of how adults deal with death, see Marc D. Angel, *The Orphaned Adult: Confronting the Death of a Parent* (New York: Human Sciences Press, 1986).

4. See Franz Borkenau, "The Concept of Death," in Robert Fulton, ed., *Death and Identity* (New York: Wiley Press, 1966), 42–56.

5. Rabbi Lamm addressed a session dealing with hospice care at the General Assembly of the Council of Jewish Federations, in Atlanta, Georgia, November 17, 1983.

6. See Nahmanides' comment on Genesis 25:8.

7. See Louis Ginsburg, *Legends of the Jews* (Philadelphia: Jewish Publication Society, 1968), 6:112–13, n. 641.

8. Ibid., 1:287–8.

9. See the responsa of Rabbi David ibn Abi Zimra, vol. 1, no. 256.

10. Elisabeth Kübler-Ross, *On Death and Dying* (New York: Macmillan, 1975).

11. Thomas, *The Lives of a Cell,* 58–9.

12. Haim David Halevy, *Asei Lekha Rav*, vol. 2 (Tel Aviv, 5738 [1977]). A lengthy discussion of the subject begins on p. 17.

Chapter 11: The Nation of Israel

1. Fernand Braudel, *The Mediterranean and the Mediterranean World in the Age of Philip II* (New York: Harper & Row, 1973), 2:826.
2. Eliyahu Benamozegh, *In Ethical Paths* [Hebrew] (Jerusalem: Mossad HaRav Kook, 1966), 28.
3. Uziel, *Mikhmanei Uziel*, 292f.
4. Ibid., 145f.
5. Ibid., 217f.
6. Ibid., 305.
7. The following material is drawn from my article "A Fresh Look at Conversion," *Midstream* (October 1983), 35–38.
8. Abraham Isaac Kook, *Da'at Kohen* (Jerusalem: Mossad HaRav Kook, 1942), 144, 155.
9. Uziel, *Mishpetei Uziel*, n. 18 and 20. See also my article "Another Halakhic Approach to Conversions," *Tradition* (Winter/Spring 1972), 107–113.
10. Yehezkel Kaufmann, *Golah veNekhar* (Tel Aviv, Devir, 1928), 1:226f.
11. Shlomo Goren, responsum printed in *Shanah beShanah* (Jerusalem, 5743 [1983]), 149–156.
12. Moshe Feinstein, *Iggrot Mosheh*, 1950, Y.D. No. 160.

Chapter 12: Family, Society, Individual

1. Margaret Mead, *Culture and Commitment: A Study of the Generation Gap* (New York: Natural History Press, 1970).
2. Emil Fackenheim, *To Mend the World: Foundations of Future Jewish Thought* (New York: Schocken Books, 1982), 250f.
3. Halevy, *Asei Lekha Rav*, 1:46–48. See also 2:139ff.
4. Elias Canetti, *Crowds and Power* (New York: Seabury Press, 1978), 178.
5. Uziel, *Mikhmanei Uziel,* 153.
6. Ibid., 458f.
7. Richard L. Rubenstein, *The Age of Triage: Fear and Hope in an Overcrowded World* (Boston: Beacon Press, 1983).

For Further Reading

Abravanel, Judah. *The Philosophy of Love*. Trans. by F. Friedeberg-Seeley and Jean H. Barnes. London: Soncino Press, 1937.

Abudraham, David ben Joseph ben David. *Abudraham haShalem*. Jerusalem, Usha Press, 5723 [1963].

Angel, Marc D. *Choosing to Be Jewish: The Orthodox Road to Conversion*. Jersey City, NJ: KTAV Publishing, 2005.

_____. *Foundations of Sephardic Spirituality: The Inner Life of Jews of the Ottoman Empire*. Woodstock, VT: Jewish Lights, 2006.

_____. *The Jews of Rhodes: The History of a Sephardic Community*. New York: Sepher-Hermon Press, 1978.

_____. *La America: The Sephardic Experience in the United States*. Philadelphia: Jewish Publication Society, 1982.

_____. *Loving Truth and Peace: The Grand Religious Worldview of Rabbi Benzion Uziel*. Northvale, NJ: Jason Aronson, 1999.

_____. *Maimonides—Essential Teachings in Jewish Faith & Ethics: The Book of Knowledge & the Thirteen Principles of Faith—Annotated & Explained*. Woodstock, VT: SkyLight Paths, 2011.

_____. *Maimonides, Spinoza and Us: Toward an Intellectually Vibrant Judaism*. Woodstock, VT: Jewish Lights, 2009.

_____. *The Orphaned Adult: Confronting the Death of a Parent*. Northvale, NJ: Jason Aronson, 1997.

_____. *Rabbi Haim David Halevy: Gentle Scholar and Courageous Thinker*. With Hayyim Angel. Jerusalem: Urim Publications, 2006.

_____. "Reclaiming Orthodox Judaism." Special issue, *Conversations: The Journal of the Institute for Jewish Ideas and Ideals* 12 (Winter 2012).

_____. "Ruminations on Sephardic Identity." *Midstream* 18 (March, 1972): 64–67.

_____. *Voices in Exile: A Study in Sephardic Intellectual History*. Hoboken, NJ: KTAV Publishing, 1991.

Azikri, Elazar. *Sefer Hareidim*. Jerusalem, 1958.

Benamozegh, Eliyahu. *In Ethical Paths* [Hebrew]. Jerusalem: Mossad HaRav Kook, 1966.

_____. *Israel and Humanity*. Trans. and ed. Maxwell Luria. New York: Paulist Press, 1995.

Braudel, Fernand. *The Mediterranean and the Mediterranean World in the Age of Philip II*. Vol. 2. New York: Harper & Row, 1972.

Canetti, Elias. *Crowds and Power*. New York: Seabury Press, 1978.

Chouraqui, André. *Between East and West: A History of the Jews of North Africa*. Philadelphia: Jewish Publication Society, 1968.

Cordovero, Moshe. *The Palm Tree of Deborah*. Trans. Louis Jacobs. New York: Vellentine, Mitchell, 1960.

_____. *Sefer Gerushin*. Shklov, 5551 [1791].

Eliade, Mircea. *The Sacred and the Profane: The Nature of Religion*. New York: Harvest Books, 1959.

Halevy, Haim David. *Aseh Lekha Rav*. 9 vols. Tel Aviv, 5736–49 [1975–88].

_____. *Mekor Hayyim*. 5 vols. Jerusalem, 5743 [1982].

Halevy, Yehudah. *The Kuzari: An Argument for the Faith of Israel*. Trans. H. Hirschfeld. New York: Shocken Books, 1968.

Ibn Pakuda, Bahya. *Duties of the Heart*. Trans. Moses Hyamson. New York: Feldheim, 1978.

Kaplan, Aryeh. *Jewish Meditation: A Practical Guide*. New York: Shocken Books, 1985.

_____. *Meditation and Kabbalah*. York Beach, ME: Samuel Weiser, 1982.

Karo, Yosef. *Sefer Magid Mesharim*. Jerusalem: Orah, 1960.

Kübler-Ross, Elisabeth. *On Death and Dying*. New York: Macmillan, 1975.

Luzzatto, Moshe Hayyim. *Da'at Tevunot* [The Knowing Heart]. Trans. Shraga Silverstein. New York: Feldheim, 1982.

_____. *Mesillat Yesharim: The Path of the Just*. 2nd rev. ed. Trans. Shraga Silverstein. New York: Feldheim, 1980.

Maimonides, Moses. *Guide of the Perplexed*. Trans. Shlomo Pines. Chicago: University of Chicago Press, 1963.

Mead, Margaret. *Culture and Commitment: A Study of the Generation Gap*. New York: Natural History Press, 1970.

Papo, Eliezer. *The Essential Pele Yoetz: An Encyclopedia of Ethical Jewish Living*. Trans. Marc D. Angel. New York: Sepher-Hermon Press, 1991.

Schechter, Solomon. *Studies in Judaism*. 2nd ed. Philadelphia: Jewish Publication Society, 1908.

Scholem, Gershom. *Major Trends in Jewish Mysticism*. Rev. ed. New York: Shocken Books, 1967.

Index

CPSIA information can be obtained
at www.ICGtesting.com
Printed in the USA
BVHW031636240321
603340BV00001B/29